Solutions for Modern Learning

Gearing Up for Learning Beyond K–12

Bryan Alexander

Solution Tree | Press

Copyright © 2016 by Solution Tree Press

All rights reserved, including the right of reproduction of this book in whole or in part in any form.

555 North Morton Street

Bloomington, IN 47404

800.733.6786 (toll free) / 812.336.7700

FAX: 812.336.7790

email: info@solution-tree.com

solution-tree.com

Visit **go.solution-tree.com/21stcenturyskills** to access material related to this book.

Printed in the United States of America

19 18 17 16 15   1 2 3 4 5

Library of Congress Control Number: 2015946560

ISBN: 978-1-942496-35-9 (perfect bound)

Solution Tree
Jeffrey C. Jones, CEO
Edmund M. Ackerman, President

Solution Tree Press
President: Douglas M. Rife
Senior Acquisitions Editor: Amy Rubenstein
Editorial Director: Lesley Bolton
Managing Production Editor: Caroline Weiss
Senior Editor: Kari Gillesse
Copy Editor: Rachel Rosolina
Proofreader: Ashante Thomas
Text Designer: Rian Anderson
Cover Designers: Rian Anderson and Abigail Bowen

Acknowledgments

Will Richardson was the inspiration for this book, taking the initiative to bring it and the others in the *Solutions for Modern Learning* series into being. He wrangled the series with grace and aplomb, while answering my many odd email queries and bringing patience to this text.

Thank you to the local public schools, which have been enormously helpful in my research. School board colleagues for the town of Ripton and the Addison County Supervisory Union, high school and elementary school teachers, administrators, support staff, parents, students, and community members have enriched this book through their reflections and generous conversations. As our state of Vermont faces major educational upheaval, your collective strength, vision, and wisdom has been an inspiration.

To my social web, I owe great and ongoing thanks. Thoughtful readers of my blog have contributed constructive comments on- and offline to posts pushing at many of this book's topics. Members of the Association of Professional Futurists challenged and inspired me. Audiences on several continents endured presentations of much of this material and graciously gave feedback.

Future Trends in Technology and Education subscribers have read and shared the monthly *FTTE* report very generously. They have also informed me every month, suggesting news stories, topics, and interpretations. You are superb, kind *FTTE* friends.

My wife and two children have each journeyed with me in the course of making this book. Ceredwyn created and co-taught an innovative flipped classroom for emergency services instruction, quietly revolutionizing that field. Gwynneth, our eldest child, has taken classes at two very different institutions and kindly answered my ruthless barrage of questions about her experiences. Owain, our youngest, has been working through high school and similarly bore up under my inquisition. To all three of you I owe not only gratitude, but my entire heart.

Table of Contents

About the Author vii

Preface ix

Introduction 1
   Revising Our Understanding of Higher Education 4
   Imagining the Future of Higher Education 5

Chapter 1: After the Technological Tsunami 9
   Our Dynamic Digital Landscape 11
   New Learning From New Technologies 13
   The Wake of New Technologies and Practices 15
   Conclusion 17

Chapter 2: The World and the Campus 19
   Changing Policies, Changing Campuses 21
   Conclusion 22

Chapter 3: Peak Campus 25
   Forces Driving Peaks and Bubbles in
      Higher Education 27
   Families and Campuses Scale the Peak 28
   Higher Education After Its Peak 30
   Conclusion 32

Chapter 4: College After Campuses 35

Informal Learning 37
Online Learning 38
Open Education 39
New Forms of Online Learning 40
Hands-On Learning 40
Conclusion 41

Chapter 5: Campus of the Future 43

Preparing for Learning After High School 44
    Making Choices About Higher Education and Other Pathways 44
    Skills for Learning Beyond K–12 46
    Considerations for Adult Learners 47
    Building Capacity for New Forms of Learning 47
Schooling in the New Gilded Age 48
    Overcoming Educational Segregation 50
Guiding Social and Technological Transformation 51
    Technology 51
    The Traditional Campus 51
    Learning Alternatives 51
    Politics 52
Conclusion 52

References 53

About the Author

Bryan Alexander is a futurist, researcher, writer, speaker, consultant, and teacher, working in the field of how technology transforms education. He completed his English language and literature PhD at the University of Michigan in 1997, with a dissertation on doppelgangers in Romantic-era fiction and poetry.

Bryan then taught literature, writing, multimedia, and information technology studies at Centenary College of Louisiana. There, he also pioneered multicampus interdisciplinary classes, while organizing an information literacy initiative.

From 2002 to 2014, Bryan worked with the National Institute for Technology in Liberal Education (NITLE), a nonprofit working to help small colleges and universities best integrate digital technologies. With NITLE, he held several roles, including codirector of a regional education and technology center, director of emerging technologies, and senior fellow. Over those years, Bryan helped develop and support the nonprofit, grew peer networks, consulted, and conducted a sustained research agenda.

In 2013, Bryan launched Bryan Alexander Consulting, LLC. Through BAC, he consults throughout higher education in the United States and abroad. Bryan also speaks widely and publishes frequently.

To learn more about Bryan's work, visit his website, http://bryanalexander.org, and follow him on Twitter at @BryanAlexander.

To book Bryan Alexander for professional development, contact pd@solution-tree.com.

Preface
By Will Richardson

In the 1960s and 1970s, Penguin published a series of what it called *education specials*, short books from a variety of authors such as Neil Postman, Ivan Illich, Herb Kohl, Paulo Freire, Jonathan Kozol, and others. All told, there were more than a dozen works, and they were primarily edgy, provocative essays meant to articulate an acute dissatisfaction with the function of schools at the time. The titles reflected that and included books such as *The Underachieving School, Compulsory Mis-Education and the Community of Scholars, Teaching as a Subversive Activity, Deschooling Society,* and *School Is Dead*, to name a few. Obviously, the messages of these books were not subtle.

Progressive by nature, the authors generally saw their schools as unequal, undemocratic, and controlling places of conformity and indoctrination. They argued, mostly to nonlistening ears, that traditional school narratives were leaving their learners disengaged and lacking in creativity and curiosity, and the systems and structures of schools were deepening instead of ameliorating the inequities in society. A number of the authors argued that universal schooling was a pipe dream from both economic and political perspectives, and schools, if they were to remain, needed to be rethought from the ground up.

Reading many of these works now, it's hard not to be struck by how precisely they describe many of the realities of today's world. It's inarguable that an education in the United States (and elsewhere) remains vastly unequal among socioeconomic groups and various races and ethnicities. The systems that drove schools years ago prevail and, in many cases, are less and less economically viable by the day. By and large, education is something still organized, controlled, and delivered by the institution; very little agency or autonomy is afforded to the learner over his or her own learning. Decades of reform efforts guided principally by politicians and businesspeople have failed to enact the types of widespread changes that those Penguin authors and many others felt were needed for schools to serve every learner equally and adequately in preparing him or her for the world that lies ahead.

It's the "world that lies ahead" that is the focus of this book, part of the *Solutions for Modern Learning* series. Let us say up front that we in no way assume that these books will match the intellectual heft of those writers in the Penguin series (though we hope to come close). However, we aspire to reignite or perhaps even start some important conversations about change in schools, given the continuing longstanding challenges from decades past as well as the modern contexts of a highly networked, technology-packed, fast-changing world whose future looks less predictable by the minute.

Changes in technology since the early 1990s, and specifically the Internet, have had an enormous impact on how we communicate, create, and most importantly, learn. Nowhere have those effects been felt more acutely than with our learners, most of whom have never known a world without the Internet. In almost all areas of life, in almost every institution and society, the effects of ubiquitously connected technologies we now carry with us in our backpacks and back pockets have been profound, creating amazing opportunities and complex challenges, both of which have been hard to foresee. In no uncertain terms, the world has changed and continues to change quickly and drastically.

Yet, education has remained fairly steadfast, pushing potentially transformative learning devices and programs to the edges, never allowing them to penetrate to the core of learning in schools. Learning in schools looks, sounds, and feels pretty much like it did in the 1970s, if not in the early 1900s.

Here's the problem: increasingly, for those who have the benefit of technology devices and access to the Internet, learning outside of school is more profound, relevant, and long lasting than learning inside the classroom. Connected learners of all ages have agency and autonomy that are stripped from them as they enter school. In a learning context, this is no longer the world that schools were built for, and in that light, it's a pretty good bet that a fundamental redefinition of school is imminent.

While some would like to see schools done away with completely, we believe schools can play a crucially important role in the lives of our youth, the fabric of our communities, and the functioning of our nations. But moving forward, we believe schools can only play these roles if we fully understand and embrace the new contexts that the modern world offers for learning and education. This is not just about equal access to technology and the Internet, although that's a good start. This is about seeing our purpose and our practice through a different lens that understands the new literacies, skills, and dispositions that students need to flourish in a networked world. Our hope is that the books in the *Solutions for Modern Learning* series make that lens clearer and more widespread.

Introduction

Skate to where the puck is going to be, not to where it has been.
—Wayne Gretsky

Today is Wednesday, which means Lucy has two classes, history and biology. She gathers up her things—phone, snack, umbrella against the likelihood of rain—and drives to campus.

Today, Modern European History isn't very crowded, much like the rest of Lucy's college courses, with eleven students scattered across a room built for thirty. She remembers high school classes as being more crowded, and picks out a seat. Lucy quickly reviews part of this week's videos concerning the Congress of Vienna (1814–1815) on her phone until the professor arrives.

This is the third class and second campus of the day for Arthur to teach. He cobbles together a living by adjuncting part-time at as many colleges and universities as he can, as do most of his colleagues and friends. Entering the classroom, Arthur takes a moment to organize his thoughts, recalling which course this is, and where in the semester they are at this point, plus the name of one student who left an especially thoughtful comment on his lectures. He's used to this kind of mental orientation practice, as he conducts it every time he shifts campus and class. It's part of being a modern academic nomad, the typical 21st century professor.

Class begins with discussion, as Lucy's peers pick up arguments they made last week and online across multiple online venues, including messaging, discussion, and blogging services. Students and adjunct explore the events of 1815, all using various devices to reference the online discussion and resources: phones, phablets, laptops, crinkly forearm displays (flexible screens attached to their sleeves, light-based keyboards projected onto desks or arms). They identify resources that confirm their insights, or challenge their classmates.' Students record or write their developing reflections, making them available for classmates to ponder and Arthur to assess. Most also throw digital content onto wall displays, using the classroom network to transfer documents from their own devices to the wall-mounted, floor-to-ceiling LCD screens. For her part, Lucy is a bit quiet, still thinking about the 1790s, as she's been playing a French Revolution massively multiplayer online game for months. The Revolution fascinates her with its powerful ideas transforming the lives of leaders and everyday French people alike. Lucy plays a lawyer from Lyons, fighting hard to preserve her city from the Terror. Several of her in-game colleagues, and one adversary, have become good out-of-game friends. Lucy's immersion in this engaging milieu has led her to a conundrum. She's still trying to figure out how Napoleon emerged on top of the revolutionary scrum, when other leaders, like Danton, had at least as much potential to lead the French nation. Back in her class, Lucy likes combining screenshots and video clips of To the Bastille! with period music and her own reflections, sharing them with classmates, thousands of fellow players, and simply interested folks. Maybe what she decides about Bonaparte's rapid rise to power can help her—and her classmates—understand the post-Waterloo political settlement.

After Modern European History, Lucy heads off campus to the city arboretum, where her Plants and People class takes place. There are no other students physically present, nor an instructor. Lucy has not met any of them in person. Instead, classwork consists of Lucy examining plants and their immediate environment, using her phone to ask questions and research. The previous week's homework (data sets, audio lectures, readings) prepared her for this arboretum class. At times, Lucy hovers her phone over a certain plant so that an app can overlay information based on Lucy's location and what the camera displays. She doesn't pay attention to other arboretum visitors, as she is focused on her work.

Biology finishes during late afternoon, and Lucy chats with her younger brother as she drives home in the gathering dusk. Jonathan has never seen the appeal of a physical campus, preferring the openness and flexibility of wholly online learning. Lucy thinks it's because he's living on his own for the first time and cherishes that independence, not wanting to be constrained by someone else's space. He disliked that *about high school and resents it at work. For his part, Jonathan thinks his older sister is just showing her age, wallowing in nostalgia for the times of crowded campuses and offline school spirit.*

Before hanging up, Lucy and Jonathan each renew their vow to finish school before the other, grinning, because they know full well they'll never really stop learning in this world.

Never has there been a better time for learning. Yet, there has never been a stranger time to be teaching.

More people than ever before have access to more information. Indeed, the sheer amount of available content has driven us to invent new terminology (yottabytes!) and new professions (data curation specialist) just to cope with the bounty. Anyone who wants to learn about a topic may face vast and growing informational riches. Learners can also connect with an ever-growing number of teachers and fellow students.

Such teachers are not necessarily so fortunate. On the positive side, they too can partake of this grand banquet of learning, which allows them to more easily stay current in their fields while branching out to new ones. However, instructors face new challenges in many areas. In some countries, the traditional school-age population (roughly five to twenty-two) is dwindling, driving colleges and universities to increasing competition for fewer pupils (Taylor, 2014). New technologies present all kinds of problems for teachers, from added workload to greater complexity (and potential embarrassment) in the classroom to the possibility of online competition. In the United States, demographics, economics, and policy pressure combine to make the teaching life more difficult all too often.

Taken together, these factors mean that higher education is changing. Colleges, universities, academies, and other postsecondary education institutions are transforming into different places from the ones we once expected. They are becoming stranger institutions than the ones teachers, scholars, administrators, and legislators experienced, planned for, or hoped to enter. Visions of higher education drawn from popular culture, adults' memories, nostalgia, or pundits are increasingly likely to be out of date, politically biased, culturally partial, simply not very useful any longer, or a combination of these.

The leap from high school to college has changed and will mutate into still more unfamiliar shapes over the next decade. High school students and their parents have more to research about college options as they examine new campus features and programs, such as learning commons, 3-D printing support and makerspaces, and mobile device policies. These students and their families will have new options for study after high school, too, including a variety of online options. Parents' own high school experiences are gradually relegated to history, while their work and personal lives provide clues to the modern college: always-on Internet access, connections through social media, a rising amount of part-time work, collaboration with distant, unmet people. Some may feel as though the transition from secondary to postsecondary education resembles science fiction, as in Vernor Vinge's classic 2006 novel about future high school, *Rainbows End*.

Revising Our Understanding of Higher Education

To be able to think seriously about higher education, we need to revise our understanding of that educational sector. We can't do otherwise if we want to realistically plan for jobs, for further education, local economies, or the continued growth of human knowledge. To paraphrase Wayne Gretzky's advice in the epigraph, we must strategize based on where higher education is likely to be going, not where it once was.

It's not an easy framework to adopt, given how many factors are in flux. Part of the appeal of Gretzky's aphorism is that it involves multiple objects sliding on ice, rather than being solidly planted on friendlier terrain, an apt metaphor for higher education's new developments. *Gearing Up for Learning Beyond K–12* approaches this slippery problem from a futures perspective. That means it draws on the forecasting field's tools of trends analysis, horizon scanning, and scenario construction.

Some of that trend analysis stems from my work on a long-term monthly publication. Since March 2012, I've published *Future Trends in Technology and Education* (*FTTE*), a report tracking developments impacting higher education in more than one hundred categories. These categories include: educational contexts, such as economics, national policy, campus policies, and demographics; technology across many domains, from hardware to software to surveillance and robotics; and the many intersections of technology and education. Over the years I've written *FTTE*, certain drivers within these categories have emerged as sustained forces, drivers most likely to shape future campuses, while others have faded into unlikelihood (Alexander, 2014a). In the following chapters, we will focus on the former, our discussion honed by a critical understanding of what happened to the latter.

This book also relies on the New Media Consortium's Horizon Project. Horizon Reports are examples of the Delphi process, a method for working with experts in a field to distill their wisdom about that field's future. Initially devised by the RAND Corporation for use by the military, the Delphi process has spread to the business world and to nonprofits (Alexander, 2009). To the best of my knowledge, Horizon is the leading research effort using Delphi for the topic of education's future. Full disclosure: I have been on the advisory board for many Horizon Reports.

The most recent Horizon Reports for higher education reveal a sector wracked by change and uncertainty. Technological forces are clearly at play, freeing up access to open education, enabling the creation of new classroom types, and altering the ways we process information. But Horizon now notes other forces at work, specifically those from the policy world. Competing demands for increased access to postsecondary education, reduced cost, more collaboration, more institutional agility, better digital skills, and a greater emphasis on teaching combine to place enormous pressures on campus leaders and staff (Johnson, Becker, Estrada, & Freeman, 2015).

It's important to keep in mind that division between technological change and change from other domains. Each can be very attractive and also exceedingly complex, drawing our attention to the exclusion of others. I find the futures approach with the daunting acronym of STEEP to be helpful in balancing these perspectives. STEEP stands for *social, technological, economic, environmental,* and *political forces.* It's a kaleidoscopic approach that helps us understand the interrelated, complex, multifaceted nature of shifts in education.

Imagining the Future of Higher Education

As befits a work drawing on the futurist tradition, this book does not guarantee certain futures or specific predictions. Instead it explores the full range of possible forms higher education might take, based on our best possible knowledge of the present. Let me expand on this point in the form of several caveats.

First, it is possible that a black swan event could disrupt higher education in ways this book does not anticipate. A *black swan* is Nicholas Taleb's term for very low probability, very high-impact occurrences, such as the sudden appearance of a black swan from a huge number of white birds. They are extraordinary events, are extraordinarily difficult to anticipate ahead of time. Ironically, we tend to change our sense of our own understanding afterward, back-filling to imagine we knew the event was actually quite predictable after all (Taleb, 2007). For the subject of this book, the appearance of affordable artificial intelligence reaching the level of a decent college tutor would constitute such a major disruption. If created for learning, a virtual entity, like the one depicted in the movie *Her* (Barnard, Farrey, & Jonze, 2013), could challenge the very structure of formal education. Another black swan would be a major terrorist attack on the United States, which leads to drastic restrictions on the Internet, on information access, the movement of populations, and public financing. All of these would alter education in sudden and deep ways. We could consider these and other extraordinary events but are limited by their low probability and by restrictions of space.

Second, *Gearing Up for Learning Beyond K–12* is focused on higher education in the United States. This is partly due to limitations of space in this volume, as addressing the sheer diversity and extent of global postsecondary education would require a great deal more text. The enormous research burden required to assess global higher education at a truly international level would require a different textual apparatus as well. I hope to address this global challenge in subsequent publications.

Third, although focusing on one country's postsecondary education system can risk excessive narrowness, the United States' higher education ecosystem is actually very rich and diverse. It includes institutions private and public, secular and of many religious affiliations, military and Quaker, community colleges and research universities. Some institutions enroll fewer than one hundred students, while others teach tens of thousands. As we explore the many different ways higher education can evolve in the next decades, bear in mind that these changes will play out across a various, even contradictory landscape.

Fourth, this book will gradually date itself as the years advance. Observations about current events become history soon enough, and technological notes risk obsolescence even more rapidly. Placing arguments in print, even in ebook form, is a risky venture. And yet I hope this will be useful during the period it describes, 2015–2025, especially in the first few years. *Gearing Up for Learning Beyond K–12* is at least a snapshot in time, a glimpse into how some of us thought about higher education in the United States during the era of President Barack Obama, onrushing climate change, the Apple Watch, Miley Cyrus, and ISIS.

Given these caveats and intentions, who is this book for? I write for everyone interested in the future of higher education. High school students picking colleges to apply to, policymakers weighing budgetary and policy demand, adult learners considering a return to university, middle school principals preparing teachers and students for the next generation, workers looking to reskill, family members seeking to help relatives succeed in the rapidly changing world of education; I hope all of you can learn from these chapters about how these places of learning develop in the future. It's vital to remember that no matter how large these issues appear, each of you will contribute to what higher education becomes.

I deliberately resisted using jargon in this book because I want it to be accessible to as wide an audience as possible. When chapters discuss technology, they do so in a nongeekish, low-acronym, gently explained way. Occasionally, Byzantine university structures and policies hit these pages under the assumption that readers are not campus administrators. Forays into economics occur without presuming readers are macro- or microeconomic gurus. The future of higher education is complex, drawing on several domains, each with its own arcana. I want to demystify that in this little book.

Gearing Up for Learning Beyond K–12 is organized chronologically. Each chapter explores colleges and universities at different points in time, starting with the present and advancing roughly into the next decade. This is a short- and medium-term future.

Chapter 1 outlines the present technological environment already at work in higher education. The details of this nearly completed revolution may surprise some readers, and show quite clearly how the 21st century classroom differs from that of the 20th. The chapter then identifies other technologies just starting to have an impact on education, analyzing their likely effects over the next few years.

Chapter 2 turns to nontechnological forces, the SEEP of STEEP after technology. These drivers will give rise to changes playing out on a longer timescale than their digital cousins, taking us across the next decade. Here we look to economics, demographics, policies, and campus strategy to see how these forces will reshape campuses.

Chapter 3 considers the possibility that higher education in the United States hit a peak in or around 2013, and has started to decline in important ways, shrinking in size and eventually cost. Alternatively, colleges and universities are around the top of a bubble cycle, with a collapse coming up fast. Either way, these arguments see decades of postsecondary education growth reversed before 2025, with enormous impact on campuses. I suggest one post-peak, post-bubble model for college, based on a university offering already existing.

Chapter 4 turns away from the storied campus of quads and residence halls to outline off-campus ways of learning at an advanced level. From hackerspaces to edupunk, informal learning to the cryptically named cMOOCs, new options are opening up for students who wish to learn without heading to a campus. Still nascent in many ways, these new academic venues will take time to build out, pushing their horizon further forward still.

Chapter 5 is a sort of coda, knitting together threads from the previous chapters then returning readers to the present. We revisit the STEEP approach to see how those forces interact and combine to influence individual decision making, then offer some additional possible futures for the contexts of higher education.

I owe a great deal to my network of friends, co-conspirators, and the occasional utter stranger who contributed insights, references, news items, and reality checks over the past few years. Much applause is due to them. In contrast, all errors of fact as well as prognostication are my own. Please contact me to crow about lapses, to offer additional information, or to share your experiences in thinking through the next decade of campus life in the United States.

Chapter 1
After the Technological Tsunami

What is technology doing to higher education?

To understand its impact, it is best to imagine a predigital university classroom in its full, nearly nostalgic glory. Let us choose the preweb date of 1985. Consider a seminar, where a professor leads a small class of a dozen or twenty students in the exploration of archaeology or Russian history. That professor is older, probably male, most likely white, and either tenured or fighting hard to get on the tenure track. He uses a chalkboard to scrawl notes, working from papers and print books. The students (tending to be around twenty years old, male, mostly white) take notes on paper using pen or pencil. Discussion happens out loud. (Andrew Delbanco [2012] offers another good example of such a historical, even nostalgic vision in *College: What It Was, Is, and Should Be*.)

Or imagine the classic lecture hall, where the same sort of faculty member holds forth in a cavernous space containing hundreds of students. The professor might use an overhead projector and acetate-based transparencies. The flow of information is mostly one way as the professor describes principles of biology or British literature. Once more, those students take notes (or should have been doing so) with the technologies of paper and pen.

We can also envision practice-oriented learning spaces, like laboratories and music studios. Again, the main players are faculty and students. Here they would have the appropriate technologies for the curriculum: a musical instrument, microscopes, chemicals.

All of these spaces have gone through changes as of this writing. Yes, academia in the United States still has labs, lecture halls, and seminar rooms. But digital technology is invading those precincts, altering the flow of information and the social dynamics, and opening classrooms to the world.

First, digital hardware appears in these rooms. Computers aren't new on campuses—indeed, many were invented and developed there—but their appearance throughout learning spaces is a recent development. Laptops appear, used by students and faculty alike. A desktop or laptop computer now connects to an elevated projector, or directly into a massive screen, replacing the classic overhead projector. The podium may sprout its own computer, like a touch screen for controlling multiple digital outputs.

Meanwhile, smaller devices have snuck in. Students and faculty may be carrying tablets: good for passing around, fine for quickly accessing information, and not so good for typing at length. They may also have either smartphones or other mobile phones. In the lecture hall and other spaces, students may also sport personal response systems, or clickers, tiny units resembling remote controls that allow quick and simple feedback to questions.

These devices connect with each other and the rest of the world through means visible and otherwise, by cables, cell phone networks, Wi-Fi, or Bluetooth. The classroom is laced with these interconnections.

This brings us to the second technological invader: software. The physical classroom replicates itself in a virtual class, the learning management system (LMS) (also course management system or virtual learning environment in Europe). These programs furnish a space for instructors to share documents with students, curate links to curricular content hosted elsewhere on the web, publish class news, host discussions, and even create a class glossary. The LMS in turn connects to a campus library's collection of digital materials, including e-reserves, ebooks, and digital finding aids. Within or outside the physical classroom, students can access the LMS to ask questions, share reflections, and work in teams.

A raft of other software now occupies the class space, often specific to a particular academic discipline. Image processing applications for arts and design classes, statistics programs for fields relying on quantitative data, composition tools for music: learning software packages are now part of the college curriculum. Other apps are more broadly used across the curriculum, like web browsers, office productivity tools (word processing, spreadsheets), and the ubiquitous PowerPoint. Some of these are networked, while others work primarily offline.

Supporting all of these are campus departments that either didn't exist a generation ago, or were far smaller than they are now. Information technology units have grown into major components of campus infrastructure. Allied to them are academic computing or educational technology groups, which help faculty deploy technology for teaching and learning. Also connected are some academic library functions, which support learning and resource management. (All of these important units are often grouped under "administration," and account for a portion of that header's growth.)

Taken together, the classrooms of 2015 have added a digital layer on top of the classrooms of, say, 1985. We experience them differently as students, instructors, and staff. Teaching and learning have been altered. Already, the digital revolution has made its mark. But all of this describes where Gretzky's puck already is. Where is the technology taking us next?

To begin answering that question, we should survey the general digital landscape of today, looking for what's starting to appear, what emerges, and what is growing.

Our Dynamic Digital Landscape

The most visible sign of new technologies is the proliferation of new devices. Mobile phones (smartphones and featurephones) are already widely used. E-readers, most notably the Kindle, have won over a substantial proportion of the reading public. Tablet devices like the iPad have made their way into a space between e-readers, phones, and laptops. Portable gaming devices, dating back to the 1990s, continue to be in play. In various forms, emerging digital technologies transform the way we interact with devices themselves, as well as with the social networks through which they connect us.

Wearable computing expands our sense of mobile devices, as fitness devices appear on our bodies—trackers attached to wrists, shoes, shirts, ears—collecting and storing data about our health and other behaviors. The 1970s-era digital wristwatch has been upgraded by the Apple Watch and similar devices. GoPro cameras, Google Glass, and other devices peer at us from users' heads. All told, we have broken up the old sites of computing on desktops and clutched the pieces to our bodies.

These new devices sometimes alter our traditional mouse-and-keyboard interface expectations. That interface, which dates back to Doug Engelbart's 1968 demo, became the primary way we interact with devices, especially desktops and laptops (Doug Engelbart Institute, n.d.). And yet it is now receding into the past, at least marginally, as new forms appear. The iPhone and Android platforms have taught us to swipe and pinch glassy surfaces. Siri, OK Glass, Cortana, and others have familiarized us with functional, even comforting, voice interfaces. Kinect for Xbox responds to our gestures, allowing our whole body to communicate wirelessly. Mouse and keyboard are now just one of several venues by which we approach computing—and each other.

For we increasingly rely on the social web to connect with each other. Social media has grown enormously from its Web 2.0 roots during the first years of the 21st century, especially 2001–2004, moving from strength to strength, taking up an ever-increasing amount of our time and digital behaviors. Twitter, Facebook, Pinterest, blogging, and other sites continue to have enormous user bases. Perhaps we should think of a time when *social media* becomes obsolete as a redundant term, and we simply refer to *media*, as the default, as social. Then we will generate a new label, such as *a*social media, for media structured to reduce or prohibit social interaction.

One of the main uses we make of social media is digital video. As social media users, we increasingly consume video content online, from Netflix streaming to Hulu to YouTube, perhaps the best candidate for a single planetary communication site. We also make videos, from quick webcam clips to massive video epics, sharing them online. We create video content in another way, as videoconferencing mainstreams through Skype, Google+ Hangouts, Apple FaceTime, and many other platforms grow in user base and improve in quality.

Social computing has also altered reading, as ebooks have become more social. Amazon Kindle users can view others' annotations and share their own. LibraryThing, Goodreads, and Amazon have become platforms for readers to publish their reviews, lists, preferences, and analyses. Print books continue to exist alongside ebooks but now have this extra social networking dimension.

Our growing presence online, and its increasing emotional and temporal investment, has also boosted our confidence in offsite storage. We are more and more comfortable storing materials in what was once called, with great fanfare, cloud computing: photos, videos, Word documents, financial data, and health information. Institutions are following consumers here more carefully, but in the same general direction.

Offline, a revolution is occurring in physical manufacturing, thanks to digital advances. 3-D printers have progressed to the point of creating machine parts, human body prosthetics, and architectural components. Printer prices have fallen while device efficiencies have risen, placing us at the cusp of a home 3-D printing revolution with echoes of the 1990s desktop publishing movement. These hardware-based changes have started to appear on campuses. Already, academic departments as diverse as classical studies, cell biology, and medicine have created objects for study or practice. As other fields catch on, perhaps we will soon think in terms of 3-D printing across the curriculum.

At a broader level, automation continues to advance. The combination of improving robotics with developments in artificial intelligence has led some analysts to speculate that we are approaching a science-fiction future where much of human labor is automated, leaving the massive social question of what to do next. Will new jobs appear to employ people, or will mass unemployment or underemployment result? Those questions are beyond the scope of this chapter, but we can look for ways the technologies behind them are starting to shape teaching and learning.

New Learning From New Technologies

The proliferation of digital devices, tools, and platforms has normalized digital technology as an important mode through which we communicate, create, and learn. Many such technologies, such as video and social media outlets, are now well established in the education sector. Many campuses now maintain one or more YouTube channels, producing and sharing content for a variety of purposes. The majority of college students in 2014 report screening digital video for and in classes (Leonard, 2015). Videoconferencing is on the rise for cases like linking ailing students with class, study abroad students with faculty back home, and connecting remote researchers with each other.

Social media other than video appears in higher education through different, complementary channels. A vibrant body of faculty and graduate students maintains blogs on or around their academic fields, like the Science Blogs community (http://scienceblogs.com) or the Crooked Timber collection of political scientists and economists (http://crookedtimber.org). (Visit **go.solution-tree.com/21stcenturyskills** to access the links mentioned in this book) Students increasingly communicate using third-party (not campus-supported) platforms, from Facebook to Yik Yak, which occasionally gives rise to controversy, often when a poster's expression collides with institutional leaders' desires. It's important to reiterate this point about faculty, students, and staff using off-campus social media. This reliance on technologies not supported by campus IT, but provided instead by third-party companies and platforms, represents a kind of academic technology outsourcing. Put another way, academics are increasingly using cloud computing to host some of their academic work, including intellectual debates, explorations, reflections, and a lot of writing.

We can see a combination of social media and web video in the spectacular rise (and ongoing crisis) of massively open online classes, or MOOCs. MOOCs appeared in 2008 amid a frenzy of media hype, accompanied by venture capital excitement and state governmental interest. They represent the possibility of educating very large numbers of people—tens or hundreds of thousands of students per single class—at very low cost. In fact, students can take the overwhelming majority of MOOCs for free, and by one estimate, the cost to campuses ranges from a mere $39,000 to more than $325,000 per class (Hollands & Tirthali, 2014). MOOCs also offer the possibility of bringing top-notch American university teaching to the entire Internet-capable population of the world, including underserved populations. However, the hype wave crashed on the rocks of several realities: the majority of students enrolling in MOOCs already have some postsecondary education and tend to be professionals; completion rates remain exceedingly low; and poor and marginalized students fared badly. Some leading MOOC providers such as Udacity have switched their attention away from academics to business training, while others such as edX and Coursera continue to explore what can be realized from these experiments. Using enormous amounts of data generated by large numbers of students to better understand how online learning works and creating a professional development function for teachers are two of the leading areas for current MOOC research and development.

So what do MOOCs have to do with social media? The leading type of MOOC, what some call the Stanford model or xMOOC (*x* as in edX, the Harvard/MIT-led MOOC provider), relies heavily on a sequence of video lectures. Learners connect through old-school discussion boards, or go around the MOOC platform to use social media. A MOOC involving tens or hundreds of thousands of learners is now possible because of the maturation of web video and web-based human interaction. On a smaller scale, web-based interaction has influenced the design and format of more traditional distance-learning classes. These often rely on similar tools, including video (or audio) lectures. Skype sessions with peers and professor are on the rise, given their power to knit together an otherwise distributed learning community.

The ready availability of web content to anyone with a web browser has helped make possible the open education movement, which involves the creation of learning materials that can be accessed by any would-be learner. The specific nature of openness differs depending on one's definition, but the overall movement encourages universal access to learning without barriers of cost. Allied to open education is the open access movement for scholarly publishing. This approach to research is based on Internet technologies for ease of access with no charge to the user. Taken together, open access and open education expand the amount of learning material available to any networked individual. Hundreds of institutions worldwide have already committed themselves to working with open education (visit Open Education Consortium at www.oeconsortium.org to learn more about such open courses and institutions). For example, Open SUNY (http://open.suny.edu) has aggregated free and open learning content for the sixty-four State University of New York colleges, universities, and institutes. This helps address student concerns about spiraling textbook costs. That content in turn supports hundreds of free, online degrees and more than 10,000 classes, which helps make postsecondary education available for the entire New York state population.

With digital access to so much information, it is not surprising that students and educators need a way to manage the sheer amount of content they produce and with which they interact. This need has given rise to the eportfolio movement. Students at participating institutions contribute digital items to these web-based holding places, including papers, presentations, posters, and art. Later in their campus careers, these students then add reflections on their growth over time. A reader (such as an employer, a grantor, or a graduate school admissions officer) can look through an e-portfolio to get a richer sense of the learner's progress and achievements. The

Association for Authentic, Experiential and Evidence-Based Learning (www.aaeebl.org) is the best organization and resource in the world for eportfolio knowledge, practice, and professional development.

Perhaps the largest digital revolution of the 21st century has challenged many of the technologies discussed so far. While e-learning platforms have largely assumed users rely on desktops and laptops, people have quickly added mobile devices to their digital repertoire. Indeed, mobile phones, e-readers, tablets, and other machines have become leading ways for many of us to interact with the digital world. This has caused a variety of problems for institutions to solve, such as translating older LMS content into new formats for smaller screens. Face-to-face campus IT departments have been developing new support strategies for the budding number of devices appearing on campus. One IT goal is being able to recommend students and staff BYOD, bring your own device. Campus spaces are covered by Wi-Fi and cell phone networks, enabling any resident or visitor to access the entire digital world while crossing the quad.

The trend toward immediate access to learning experiences has inspired campuses to support other forms of hands-on work, as well. The maker movement, the drive to get people creating with practical materials, has found some interest in higher education. Makerspaces provide materials and instruction in woodworking, knitting, robotics, plastics, cloth, and other analog materials. Campuses as far apart as Stanford University and Mount Holyoke College have set up makerspaces for students and staff to set their hands to wood, plastics, yarn, and tin. Digital technology does appear here, occasionally as content (robotics, for example), but more often as a source of information when peer tutors aren't available on site.

The Wake of New Technologies and Practices

After so many of these technologies and practices have begun to appear in colleges and universities, faculty and staff have reacted in several ways that go beyond the specific devices. First, faculty in history, literature, classical studies, the arts, and related fields have launched the digital humanities movement. This integration of technology with classic academic inquiry began in the research university world, as professors, librarians, and technologies collaborated to create academically rigorous digital projects, including the web-based Walt Whitman Archive (www.whitmanarchive.org), the Rossetti Archive (www.rossettiarchive.org), the William Blake Archive (www.blakearchive.org), the Perseus Digital Library Project (www.perseus.tufts.edu/hopper/#) for classical studies, and the Valley of the Shadow (http://valley.lib.virginia.edu) as a U.S. Civil War resource. As digital humanities projects have grown in number and audience, the movement has migrated to other institutions, as faculty use content in classes and start producing their own. The

University of Richmond, for example, created an innovative historical mapping site, Visualizing Emancipation (http://dsl.richmond.edu/emancipation), which lets users explore the spatial and temporal distribution of slavery's end in the U.S. Civil War. A University of Mary Washington class met online with students from three other campuses in two nations to study Walt Whitman's writing using the Walt Whitman Archive. Digital humanities projects proliferate, scholarship appears, graduate students shape their studies along these lines, and grants support new work (Gold, 2012).

Second, some professors have redesigned their classes to take advantage of blended learning. This involves shifting in-class lectures to out-of-class assignments via digital video or audio recordings, replacing them in class with more discussion and hands-on work. As in K–12 classrooms, some refer to this as a flipped class, with traditional homework occurring in the class and the classic lecture transported to homework. While some classes and instructors have traditionally structured class design in this manner—think of humanities seminars, for example—it represents a pedagogical shift toward greater interaction. For some campuses, blended learning also represents a response to the challenge of distance learning: integrating the best of the digital and face-to-face worlds without heading entirely online.

Third, we have just experienced the rise of educational entrepreneurship. A number of business start-ups emerged from academia, while others appeared from outside, aimed at serving educational needs. Many of these emphasize technology, either as problem to be solved or as tool to help address other issues. For example, Remind (www.remind.com) seeks to improve student-teacher communications by developing secure mobile messaging services (Singer, 2015). Duolingo (www.duolingo.com) is a stand-alone language teaching program that draws heavily on computer gaming, and won millions of dollars in financing ("Kleiner Perkins," 2014).

Fourth, faculty members have taken to resisting their institutions' use of technology either as individuals or through departments and larger bodies. These criticisms often focus on the perceived threat of some form of distance learning to the academic enterprise and the professoriate. For example, faculty at San Jose State University famously rejected their institution's implementation of a MOOC sourced from Harvard because it represented a lower-quality learning experience than they could provide. The MOOC's video lectures would be unresponsive to students, unlike an in-person lecturer. Moreover, outsourcing part of class instruction could lead to a reduction in the number of faculty, with one MOOC replacing many instructors (Department of Philosophy, San José State University, 2013). Those fears did not materialize, although the number of tenured faculty continues to decline for non-MOOC-related reasons. However, concerns about digitally-mediated teaching being of lower quality than face-to-face persist. A 2015 Gallup poll shows many Americans regarding wholly online learning as of lesser quality than education offered by both four- and two-year institutions (McCarthy, 2015).

If we take a step back and look at higher education as a whole, we can see campuses already mutating under the impact of various technological forces. Consider, for example, Grand Valley State University (GVSU), which showcases many different digital teaching practices its faculty deployed over a year. Professors use virtual reality headsets, gesture-based computing, 3-D printing, Google Glass, and telepresence robots. Virtual reality and 3-D printing allow students to better visualize objects otherwise inaccessible from the classroom or difficult to grasp, and to exercise their creativity. Google Glass enables instructors to record tutorial videos hands-free. GVSU students could use telepresence robots for virtual tours, or to connect with off-site students ("Atomic Object," 2015). Compare this approach with the University of Washington, which maintains a research and teaching office devoted to innovating new forms of digital visualization (http://idl.cs.washington.edu). Or contrast with Broward College, which lets any student, instructor, or staff member bring to campus and use whichever mobile device he or she prefers (Weldon, 2014). Flipped classrooms have appeared across the United States, from Massachusetts to Texas (Hough, 2014; Weaver, 2014).

Conclusion

Classrooms, pedagogies, campus spaces, access to knowledge, our relationship with tangible objects, the nature of support departments, and communication on- and off-campus have all been transformed. More emergent technologies are likely to keep driving these changes over the next few years.

Yet none of these digital changes occur in a vacuum. The social, economic, and policy contexts that situate the technologies and transform and are transformed by them are the subject of the next chapter.

Chapter 2
The World and the Campus

To understand the nontechnological forces coming to bear on higher education, we can return to the nostalgic image that opened chapter 1. Recall the pre–World Wide Web classrooms of professor and students. Lectures and discussions, lab work, and music practice occurred with analog, not digital, technologies. Faculty tended to be tenure track. Students tended to be white males. The typical student age was eighteen to twenty-two years old.

The situation has changed somewhat, and is likely to change still further in the medium-term future. Now we can turn to the remaining STEEP factors, the social, technological, economic, environmental, and political currents of change. We have already addressed technology in chapter 1; now we consider the other factors.

We can begin with the social dimension and start with demographics. Predicting the future is usually a tricky proposition at best, but population patterns offer one of the least chaotic guides to what comes next. Demographic changes are often long term, due to the extreme unlikelihood of altering basic details for populations in the tens or hundreds of millions. We can extrapolate demographics with greater confidence than, say, technological or cultural trends.

Demographics in the United States are in an unusual situation, due to the relative decline of the population of people under age eighteen. Young people now make up a smaller proportion of the United States than ever before, especially in the Northeast and Midwest ("Changing patterns," 2014; Lorin, 2014a, 2014b). Birthrates have dropped for various reasons, including greater education rates, increasing material wealth, and cultural shifts. Birthrates are likely to remain low, too, as fewer people had children during the Great Recession in the mid-2000s, and people in their twenties have delayed having children (Khazan, 2014). At the same time, the senior population has grown, thanks to medical advances and the baby boomer generation entering retirement. Elders may soon constitute the largest age group in the United States, a number in rough equivalence with teens and children. This pattern is very unusual for human societies historically, but this aging population model is increasingly seen in other industrial nations, such as Japan. There may be profound implications for culture, economics, and policy.

At the same time, a racial shift is occurring as the proportion of U.S. citizens who are white declines and as the nonwhite population grows. The United States will soon become a minority-majority nation. As with the aging demographic change, this racial transformation could reshape the United States culturally and politically.

While these social changes occur, economic forces are simultaneously altering U.S. life. We experience these very personally in the world of work, where late 20th century labor conditions have given way to what some call the *gig economy*. Labor unions, once enormously important, have become scarce, especially in the private sector. The career model of one worker, one job, and one employer for life now resembles one person, several jobs, multiple employers, sometimes simultaneously. The proportion of eligible workers actually employed has been declining, too—not just from the Great Recession's unemployment spike, but from people removing themselves from the workforce through various means such as early retirement, school, and disability (Bureau of Labor Statistics, 2015).

Obviously, this emerging world of work changes our assumptions about many aspects of labor, from individual self-worth to retirement planning. These include the life and career paths high school students (and their parents) anticipate. Instead of selecting a single vocation for decades to come, teens must now prepare themselves to obtain multiple skillsets and aptitudes, to be used and developed off and on across a diverse work experience. Perhaps high school students will anticipate unusual combinations of academic preparation, like dance and business administration, woodworking and Spanish language. Such binaries are well known in the small liberal arts niche, and might become mainstream as the world of work changes.

Allied to this transformed labor situation is the dynamic of increasing economic inequality. As economists Emmanuel Saez and, more famously, Thomas Piketty show, an escalating share of U.S. income and wealth have settled around the upper one percent of earners (Piketty, 2014; Saez & Piketty, 2006). This is a relatively recent development for a county that experienced lower inequality from World War II through 1980, and one that echoes economic patterns last seen during the late nineteenth century's Gilded Age or the Roaring Twenties. Below that one percent, the middle class is both shrinking numerically and not gaining economically. Lower on the economic ladder, compensation has either stagnated or actually declined over the past generation for non-middle-class workers. Political and cultural fallout from this new Gilded Age already include the Occupy movement and a resurgence of progressive politics. As of this writing, economic inequality has become a banner issue for the 2016 presidential election.

Changing Policies, Changing Campuses

Presidential education politics have also changed, as have political approaches to higher education at the state level. It is well known that state appropriations to public universities and colleges have declined from the 1980s through the first decades of the 21st century, reaching levels low enough to elicit successive tuition rises from what used to be inexpensive institutions. Rising tuition has driven more students to pay for their education through loans, the total amount of which passed $1.2 trillion in 2014 (Board of Governors of the Federal Reserve System, 2014).

Both Democrats and Republicans have mounted parallel efforts to reform the entire education system, from primary through postsecondary levels. Drives for accountability, lower costs, better results, and better international standings have come from political leaders across the ideological spectrum. As of this writing, the Obama administration is preparing two separate ratings systems to measure college and university outcomes and operations, to the intense dislike of many campus leaders (Field, 2015).

One result of all of these combined forces is a decline in the number of students enrolled in U.S. postsecondary education. In other words, in addition to the demographic problem of a shrinking pool of *available* students, the *actual* number of enrolled students has declined overall since 2012 ("REPORT: Current Term Enrollment," 2015). The decline has been most pronounced in the for-profit sector but has also been felt in community colleges, state universities, and even to a degree in private four-year institutions. Within the population actually enrolling, the majority consists of women rather than men. For example, 27 percent of millennial women have at least a bachelor's degree, as compared with 21 percent of men (Patten & Fry, 2015). This represents a reversal of the historical pattern, which persisted up until the late 20th century.

How have campuses responded to these diverse and massive pressures on their traditional forms? In part, they act like businesses by diversifying their markets. The reduction in the traditional college-age population has led some campuses to expand their adult education offerings, often online. They also compete more fiercely for a dwindling U.S. market of eighteen to twenty-two year olds with ever more desirable on-campus amenities.

U.S. universities have made one massive effort to control costs by replacing full-time, tenured faculty with part-time or adjunct instructors. The latter cost a fraction of what the former usually receive on a per-class basis. When campuses were growing their student bodies, this allowed for a less expensive way to expand class offerings. In the post-2012 era of stagnant or declining enrollments, adjuncts help keep costs down. Unfortunately, this has meant blighted careers for many newly minted PhDs and EdDs seeking tenure or even full-time employment and its attendant compensation and support. The adjunct, not the tenure-track professor, is now the typical higher-education instructor.

Recruiters have also turned to or enhanced their focus on international markets, including Europe, North Africa, and especially south and east Asia. Some of those regions have growing teenage populations. Others suffer from high levels of income inequality, which can produce academically proficient teenagers with wealthy families—a very attractive target for college recruiters.

Campuses are concerned with improving the success rates of students as well. This has led to, among other things, the development of new ways to certify learning other than with class grades. Some are experimenting with badges, which are digital assertions of competency in a specific area. Badges may recognize skills not taught by a university class, perhaps because the topic is too narrow (such as database programming for mobile devices) or interstitial (group-work facilitation, for example). Higher education is also looking to recognize lifelong learning through competency-based learning. This approach awards credit for learning achieved beyond the academic system and can be determined through exams.

On a more negative level, campuses can consider what I've called a *queen sacrifice*. The term refers to a chess move, when one player makes the desperate move of giving up his or her queen in order to win the game. Academic institutions have a similar tactic available in challenging times, at least metaphorically. This involves cutting or drastically reducing an academic program and removing faculty who teach it (including tenured professors) and staff who support it in the service of reducing costs. Targeted programs often enroll fewer students than other parts of the curriculum. They also tend to be drawn from the humanities, although not exclusively. I refer to this as a queen sacrifice because such cuts strike the most important elements of campuses: their teaching and researching faculty, and the curriculum they support.

Campus leaders have other options for responding to these challenges, but few have selected them. One such option is reducing compensation for senior administrators, whose salaries often elicit faculty or public criticism. Another would be to cut back on varsity athletics, since the supermajority of those programs do not produce net income for their institutions (Shulman & Bowen, 2002). Few institutions have followed these courses, however, no doubt for reasons of political infeasibility.

Conclusion

In current classrooms, students are diverse. One or more are from other countries. More than half are women. Some have won credit for knowledge won through work or life experience. Some, if not many, hope the class will contribute to a degree that will win them a place in the shrinking middle class, or at least help them take care of the debt incurred by taking this very degree. Some are working part- or even full-time. Several have taken online classes, possibly from a different school, institution, or organization. The professor standing before them is a part-time adjunct, lacking an office on campus and a name on the course schedule. That instructor is likely teaching classes at other institutions at the same time and will have to drive off to the next campus, or to a relatively quiet place to teach an online class.

This typical scenario has the virtue of simplicity, but it loses sight of institutional variety. The elite liberal arts class, for example, is still probably being taught by a full-time, tenure-track professor, though that creature is far rarer in the community college setting. The professor's scholarship counts for a great deal in a research university.

I've left off professional and graduate classes. They are similar to the undergraduate classrooms I described, but without adjuncts teaching grad students. Worse yet, this scenario covers a face-to-face class, disregarding wholly online programs. Still, the single image can embrace a great number of contributory forces.

And yet this clear picture of change is not completely clear for another reason. The scenario does not represent the classroom of the future but a portrait of an institution in transition. The pre–World Wide Web classroom of 1985 is our starting point. The classroom of 2015, warped by technological and other forces of change, is a midpoint on the journey away from it. The outcomes of seriously transformed education are the subject of the next chapters.

Chapter 3
Peak Campus

Now that we have covered a variety of trends impacting higher education, from technology to economics and politics, we can select and combine a group of them that interact with each other to form a kind of megatrend. For this chapter we can pull together forces that suggest a smaller future for academics in the United States, following an experience akin to the 2008 housing bubble: peak higher education.

When I first wrote about this megatrend, the concept seemed somewhat perverse (Alexander, 2013, 2014a, 2014b). It was five years after the terrible financial crash of 2008, which kicked off what many call the Great Recession and clobbered many campuses' finances. Recovery had been under way, though, with endowments returning, charitable donations rising, and institutional cash flows largely resurrected. Very fiscally conservative, austere education spending strategies that had taken hold of state and federal governments had elicited opposition and active dislike, leading North Dakota and California to start reinvesting in their public universities. The economic argument for higher education—the college premium of a lifetime earning boost due to receiving a degree—was still popular. Also popular was American higher education abroad, as more international students continued to arrive on this country's campuses, even after the War on Terror's tightened travel restrictions. Casting a pall over this view must have seemed willfully obtuse, even offensive.

But other trends and data drove me to create an opposing view. I am not certain that what follows will transpire. Many social media commentators support it, and countervailing arguments do not demolish it. Indeed, to my surprise I have found somber support for my hypothesis from nearly every academic audience I've spoken to or otherwise communicated with, regardless of institutional type, regional identity, campus financial health, or organizational mission. The clear majority of responses to my *Inside Higher Ed* article, "Has Higher Ed Peaked?," support my outlook, or saw it as not gloomy enough (Alexander, 2014b).

Readers may be familiar with peak models, such as peak car or the now-unpopular peak oil concept. These are based on either supply or demand ascending for a time, then declining. With cars, we have seen generations of eager Americans buying one or multiple vehicles, taking the automobile dearly into our hearts, until the rising millennial population has eased off the gas and preferred other forms of transportation. With oil, supply is the problem. Peak oil held that civilization started off with the oil that was easiest to obtain, the kinds that gushed quickly to the surface or lurked in vast, accessible reservoirs. Over time producers exhausted that supply, and had to spend more to obtain the more difficult oil and gas: farther away from distribution points, deeper underground, harder to pry out from the earth. The peak here is the halfway point between discovering and exhausting planetary petroleum reserves.

Peak education follows this curve, and starts from the historical record of general increases in college enrollment. In the 18th century and the first half of the 19th century, academia was for the socioeconomic elite, a small slice of the early republic's population. But the Civil War–era Morrill Act set up a framework for many new universities and colleges, the land grant institutions. This expanded the number of students who would take classes, and also the size of the staff teaching and supporting them. World War II saw the G.I. Bill, which sent decades of Americans to college or university. The second half of the 20th century saw a veritable collegiate boom as governments, activists, and then campuses sought historically underserved or banned groups, including women, racial minorities, first-generation college students, and poor people, with overlaps across the categories. This was the era of creating more and new types of postsecondary institutions, like Hampshire College, which avoids grades in favor of written assessments. Community colleges boomed as the Cold War surged and then ended. By the end of the century, the United States was convinced, more or less, that a college degree was excellent for everyone, and the university experience was the next logical step for high school graduates and adult learners alike. Institutions grew to meet this side, building out teaching and research faculty, administrators, and support staff.

That is what things look like on the way to a peak, before we rise over the top and slide down the other side. We could also view this state of affairs as akin to a bubble's climax. Some readers will be more familiar with the bubble concept thanks to the role played by the housing bubble in 2008's financial meltdown. As with a peak curve, a bubble sees demand rising, leading to increased prices, as per the laws of supply and demand. When the bubble reaches a crescendo, price and demand deflate.

Forces Driving Peaks and Bubbles in Higher Education

To begin, U.S. higher education continues to experience a cost/value crisis, especially at the undergraduate level. Published tuition rates continue to rise faster than any other cost, even including health care (Kurtzleben, 2013), which is unusually inflationary in the United States, compared with OECD (Organisation for Economic Co-operation and Development) nations. Most students and their families do not actually pay "list price," as a mixture of grants, loans, and awards reduces the amount they owe. Nevertheless, the actual payment amounts are high, and popular perceptions are quite anxious. At the same time, scholarship and popular media offer frequent criticisms of higher education's value. The most powerful of these is the book *Academically Adrift*, which argues that a disturbingly large proportion of college graduates enter their junior and senior years having learned relatively little (Arum & Roksa, 2011).

One reason for those increasing costs is changes in the students attending college. An increasing number of undergraduates are first-generation students, who sometimes require more academic support or remediation than students from university-experienced families. Another sector of the student body brings learning disabilities, often associated with poverty or poor health, which similarly increases on-campus support budgets. Meanwhile, learners and their families have escalated their expectations for student life, and have found institutions willing to meet those demands in the form of the so-called amenities arms race. Residence halls (it's bad form to refer to them as *dorms* now) are ever more elaborate structures approaching good apartment buildings or better. Other structures to make life less onerous have also appeared on campuses, from ever-richer cafeterias to wellness centers, climbing walls, indoor rafting, and more. Private institutions have relied on increasing tuition, hiring adjuncts instead of tenure-track faculty, and the occasional endowment draw to compete in the amenities race. Public universities and colleges have had to run faster to catch up, as it were, given cuts to state funding.

To sum up, U.S. campuses may have started teaching fewer students, and those they do instruct have become more costly to serve. Put another way, the United States has overshot its carrying capacity for the higher education population, and our institutions are scrambling for strategic responses.

As we increasingly see higher education's value tied to its economic rewards, our anxiety about that value rises with concerns about graduate employment. That concern grows even further when matched to fears of excessive student debt. Roughly two-thirds of students now carry debt—and for an amount averaging roughly thirty thousand dollars. Recall that such debt cannot be discharged by bankruptcy and can be passed on to heirs upon the holder's death. News media are fond of stories that combine these fears, such as featuring a twenty-something graduate working as a Starbucks barista while barely scratching her six-figure student loan (Combe, 2013). There is a current of thought that holds that college costs more than it used to, costs more than it should, and delivers less than it promised. This is the psychology of a bubble just before it bursts.

Graduate programs are not immune from this. Several fields are facing into strong headwinds, especially law. Law schools have seen student numbers (and hence tuition dollars) drop steadily since 2010, as legal jobs have been drying up. Some law schools have responded by encouraging senior faculty to leave, by trying harder to win students from a shrinking pool, and even giving up requiring the LSAT exam. Law, once a durable career option for many undergraduates, has become instead a field in crisis (Kitroeff, 2015).

Adding to this sense of crisis is the bipartisan political pressure I spoke of in chapter 2. Before the Great Recession, educators were able to rely on governmental support from the Democratic Party. Those politicians reliably resisted Republican anti-education measures. But 2008 to 2015 have seen Democrats, most notably the Obama administration, make their own calls for education reform, which has led a long campaign to keep college tuitions low while attempting to measure their outcomes. Democratic governors and mayors across the country have applied pressure to K–12 and higher education alike, such as Chicago's mayor Rahm Emanuel (President Obama's former chief of staff) warring against that city's teachers unions. The upshot is that the political system is united in pressuring education to improve, and has many sources of pressure to apply. Each political party sometimes emphasizes different strategies for improvement, as when the Democrats urge a new college rating system and the Republicans support for-profit institutions. But neither is committed to defending higher education's status quo.

Families and Campuses Scale the Peak

The preceding list of forces would be only theoretical without evidence of people changing their behavior on the ground. That evidence has appeared.

As noted earlier, the total number of American students enrolled in colleges and universities in the U.S. has declined since 2012, even though the overall population increased. The year 2013 saw the number of students in for-profit and community colleges go down in absolute terms, while other sectors experienced plateaus or tiny increases (Pérez-Peña, 2013). In 2013, college admission officers reflected that they had a difficult time meeting even baseline recruitment targets (Jaschik, 2013). Undergraduate enrollment dropped, and so did graduate numbers (Erickson, 2013; Gonzales, Allum, & Sowell, 2013). The demographic changes we discussed in chapter 2 are starting to play a role in this dynamic, as fewer eighteen-year-olds exist to graduate from high school and start postsecondary education. This is especially evident in Midwestern and northeastern regional and local-serving institutions, as those areas are seeing the sharpest decline in the teenage population.

Simultaneously, the amount of money Americans actually spent on higher education stabilized rather than grew in accordance with rising prices (Kiley, 2013). Some students and families have downshifted their institutional choice to save money and reduce debt, selecting a community college instead of a state university, or a state school instead of a prestigious research university. Other students have reduced costs by attending local campuses and living at home instead of paying for residential life; consider them pre-graduation boomerang learners. Still others take classes from online providers instead of those with elaborate physical campus presences, which can be less of an experience for some. Some combine these—think of a learner living at home, using a laptop in the living room to interact with instructors and fellow students when not at work or caring for a family member.

Banks have already recognized these signs of the changing educational landscape and reacted. Several have withdrawn from the student loan market, seeing that field shrinking (Finkle & Peters, 2012). Wells Fargo has seen student loan yields steadily decline (Perez, 2015). Bank of America may sell its student loan operations (Scully, 2015). These are not signs of a growing field.

Meanwhile, college graduates—and those who leave school without a diploma—have entered an economic environment more challenging than any in generations. Setting aside media panic stories, we know that students in their twenties make less money than did their peers in preceding decades. They have fewer savings, are more burdened with debt, and are therefore less likely to buy a car and house than their predecessors at the same point in their respective lives. They delay getting married and having children. This has negatively impacted the economy by somewhat reducing housing and automobile demand. And it is likely to lead to another smaller generation, given fewer children are birthed later in life. Is it any wonder that rising teenagers see their elder cousins struggle and strategize ways to reduce the pain?

There are good nonpeak or nonbubble reasons we could offer to explain why fewer people are enrolling in higher education. Economic recovery is the most evident, as unemployment has gradually reduced from its Great Recession depths. Would-be workers who sought school as an alternative to and as better preparation for a hostile labor market can now leave campus to seek employment with better odds. Older adult learners could have chosen an alternative path of retirement, exiting both the workforce and formal education. And yet we cannot discount the popular anxiety about education, nor can campus leaders afford to not think about these behaviors, no matter the cause.

The specter of peak higher education and the higher education bubble sheds light on some strategies currently deployed by those campus leaders. Some of these involve reducing campus operations. At the largest scale, campus closings are perhaps the starkest response to dropping student numbers, especially for tuition-driven schools. Campus mergers are another major reaction, seeking to achieve some economies of scale by combining faculty and staff. Reducing or terminating academic programs, including their faculty and support staff, is an option when leaders perceive those units as not enrolling enough students. This is what I referred to as a queen sacrifice, and we now see it in a new light through the peak education context. The human costs in terms of jobs lost, careers blunted, and lives thrown off track are obvious, yet rarely appreciated.

More constructive options are also on the table. The flip side of a queen sacrifice is shunting additional resources (money, time, personnel, technology, and physical plants' responsibilities of maintenance and infrastructure) to programs enrolling high numbers of students, or launching new academic units for the same purpose. These may include STEM disciplines, gaming, health services, business, hospitality, and criminal justice, to name a few leading candidates. Aggressively courting international students is also a peak strategy, supplementing American shortfalls with foreign populations. Using data analytics to more assiduously market and obtain prospective learners is likely to occur and helps explain the sudden academic awareness of those tools. Ramping up the amenities arms race is another apparently viable way to more energetically fight for a share of a dwindling population.

None of these strategies have certain outcomes. Each is a kind of gamble. This year's desired academic field may become overblown next year (again, recall when law was a booming career path). Graduate students risk a great deal in guessing which field and subfield will receive resources years down the road. Campus stakeholders may or may not react negatively to changes to what they remember fondly. They might enjoy seeing greater ethnic and national diversity, or come to resent their alma mater becoming "a finishing school for the superrich of Asia" (DeLong, 2013).

Higher Education After Its Peak

These strategies might help individual campuses, but will they solve the broader problem of peak U.S. higher education? It's possible they can stave off the worst effects, if international students and migrant learners supplement the decline of the national under-nineteen population. A return to deep, sustained economic growth could inspire states to return to older levels of public university funding. A more equitable distribution of growth's spoils could reinvigorate the middle class, working synergistically with easier access to higher education.

On the other hand, powerful forces could ensure that post-peak academia suffers serious challenges. Income inequality appears to be deepening, and work by Piketty (2014) argues that it will accelerate as income differentials become wealth-based strata. Many nations from whom campuses in the U.S. wish to attract students are reforming and expanding their own academic capacity, most notably China. The challenges of teaching students needing greater support show no signs of simply going away. And there is no clear solution to the rising tuition problem. This in turn gives institutions even greater incentives to rely on more adjunct faculty, rather than creating tenure lines.

If what higher education is experiencing is really a bubble, then we could see tuition and fees start to go down, perhaps precipitously. There is certainly widespread public appetite for a price decline. It is difficult to imagine a way for tuition to fall, short of massive governmental subsidies, such as the one asked for by Vermont senator Bernie Sanders (Stratford, 2015). Preexisting campus expenses—tenured faculty compensation, administrative and staff salaries, maintaining a physical plant—are simply too large and deeply laid.

We can imagine an alternative campus that might offer significantly less expensive prices. I think of this as the Math Emporium model, inspired by a Virginia Tech service (www.emporium.vt.edu). On the Virginia Tech campus is an enormous computer lab, built in a space originally designed as a department store. This technology-enabled space was designed to help students suffering with mathematics issues, especially at the basic level. Each computer runs a suite of mathematics programs, from tutorials to statistics software. Computers sit on furniture well designed for multiple configurations, allowing learners to work on their own with some privacy or to team up for group work.

The Emporium is not entirely automated. Staff members, drawn from graduate and undergraduate students, are onsite and on call. Learners stuck on a problem can summon help from these ad hoc teachers but can, and often do, work on their own. It's a combination of homework space, tutorial, and group study hall (Robinson & Moore, 2006). Students tend to improve their mathematics understanding, shown by growth in scores and pass rates (de Vise, 2012). And costs are lower, as fewer and less-expensive staff are involved. This Virginia Tech pilot has inspired similar services on other campuses, such as one at Austin Community College (Fain, 2015).

Imagine, as a thought experiment, the Math Emporium deployed across the curriculum. Students work from the huge and growing amount of online materials, some selected by faculty members. When they need in-person help, they enter either a physical space like at Virginia Tech, or they make an appointment to meet at another location. Exams can occur through onsite or remote proctoring. Given the sheer range of online materials available, students wouldn't have to physically attend an emporium site unless they needed the option of face-to-face interaction.

It's not the idyllic college image, but it's one that could present lower costs and therefore appeal to cost-conscious students, families, and policymakers on those grounds. Perhaps a student would take classes at a traditional campus part time and others at an emporium simultaneously or alternate years at each, transferring credits. Some students could spend years in an emporium. If frustration with higher education reaches bubble levels, this might be a useful alternative.

Conclusion

At times in U.S. history (for example, the 1960s and 70s) many students went to campuses to discover themselves, to explore the meaning of life, to seek without economic constraints. That image combines with the lovely, history-saturated type of campus favored by some east coast schools and many Hollywood movies to produce a nearly romantic vision. Yet we now live in different times. The debt-fueled, post–Cold War boom is over, ended by the worst financial crisis in generations, and followed by what many refer to as the Great Recession. As I write this in the spring of 2015, U.S. economic growth is meager, creating poorly paying jobs. The classic undergraduate population (aged eighteen to twenty-two) is starting adulthood facing serious financial challenges. Attending college is a serious, necessarily self-interested, and even risky endeavor. Romantic visions of ivy-lined quads may not serve this generation well. Its elders, adult learners, are even less likely to view college in this light, being already in the midst of life, commuting to campus, and interested in how to fit classes within a life already occupied by work and family.

It is possible that this sober attitude could sour, at least for some, into a rejection of higher education. Imagine the economy continuing to shamble through low growth and stagnant compensation, what some economics term a "secular stagnation" (Summers, 2014). Assume that college and university tuition continues to rise, as does student debt. Assume, too, that mainstream news sources continue to churn out anxiety-breeding stories about all of these, with intermittent exaggerations. Some would-be learners might decide the investment is not worth the risk. Those refuseniks could inspire others. Campus leaders would have to try ways to win them back to school, including lowering tuition, somehow. We have already seen a series of well-received tuition freezes; those could inspire actual cuts. This may be how a higher education bubble bursts.

It is also possible that post-peak U.S. higher education will simply become smaller and scale back the size of campuses as well as campus spending, resources, and staffing. Post-peak academia will have fewer students, more adjunct faculty, fewer tenured professors, and many institutions owning less wealth and more debt. We have already seen campuses merge and even close, suggesting a post-peak landscape of fewer institutions. Some campuses could be physically smaller after leasing or selling land or buildings for funds. Much as the housing market remained smaller than its 2007 peak for some time, postsecondary education could occupy fewer dollars and people for a time.

Perhaps we will see would-be learners choosing options other than campuses for their education. Chapter 4 examines such possibilities for postsecondary education beyond campus walls.

Chapter 4
College After Campuses

Is it possible to learn at a university level without attending a campus?

It is certainly doable, and the options for this kind of learning are growing. But we should start our examination of this idea by looking at rationale, rather than method. Why would one pursue advanced learning off-campus?

Adult learners offer the first answer. These nontraditional students often have to juggle competing schedules and demands in order to make it to physical classes. Many have dependents, partners, or others to care for. Some (a decreasing amount, given workforce participation trends) have jobs, and their work schedules may not easily accommodate additional demands. After all, classes and transportation may take up a significant amount of time. Full-time or even part-time education simply might not fit.

The other demands of the traditional brick-and-mortar college may also present a bad fit for adults. Politicians and academic leaders present higher education as a reskilling opportunity for underemployed, unemployed, or simply ambitious adults, but campuses do not necessarily meet those needs. For example, professionally minded adults may resist an undergraduate core curriculum as extraneous to their needs. Others may value a narrow curricular band within a larger set of requirements, and wanting only the former, resent the latter. Moreover, older learners may feel awkward around younger students, based on life-stage differences.

Learners of all ages may have one additional anti-campus reason in common: a dislike of schooling. Academics sometimes forget just how deeply K–12 students fear or hate the educational experience and how those emotions can carry on beyond high school (or whenever a person exits the system). Experiences with hated classes can tar the entire institution and create severe aversions, such as mathematics phobia, most famously (or notoriously). Encounters with nonparental authority figures, bureaucracy, bullies, cliques, and the all attendant pains of growing through adolescence do not always fill one with a desire to repeat them.

For traditional-age learners, undergraduate education may not fit their emotional, developmental, or practical situations. We can all readily think of people who entered college at eighteen without any academic curiosity, or who sought real-world experiences instead of the classroom. Some may do better working full-time instead of taking classes. Others could learn much from service. For all these groups, postsecondary education may be an example of misdirection, a diversion of precious time and resources. They could be better served by delaying university until their situations have shifted to be more supportive of academic study.

The employment issue is especially significant. If the U.S. economy sees the middle class dwindle and the working and lower classes expand, more families will experience financial need. That otherwise college-bound eighteen-year-old may be needed at home to help provide for his or her family. One sign of that class transformation is the nature of growing job types. According to the federal Bureau of Labor Statistics (2014), the fields likely to experience the most rapid growth are usually those requiring little, if any, higher education.

- Personal care aides
- Registered nurses
- Retail salespersons
- Home health aides
- Combined food preparation and serving workers, including fast food
- Nursing assistants
- Secretaries, medical secretaries, and administrative assistants, except legal, and executive
- Customer service representatives
- Janitors and cleaners, maids and housekeeping cleaners
- Construction laborers
- General and operations managers
- Laborers and freight, stock, and material movers, handymen
- Carpenters
- Bookkeeping, accounting, and auditing clerks
- Heavy and tractor-trailer truck drivers
- Office clerks, general
- Childcare workers
- Licensed practical and licensed vocational nurses

Out of this list, only registered nurses require completion of an undergraduate degree. An eighteen-year-old facing such a job market may well decide to skip university and get working, or at least delay returning to school until after accumulating some savings and work experience. The specter of debt, well displayed by mass media, could help goad such a decision.

Taken together, these reasons for not going to college could combine to reduce interest in higher education, triggering the bubble or peak scenario outlined in chapter 3.

But if high school graduates, working adults, and other potential students choose to not set foot on a campus, how can they partake of higher education's benefits?

Informal Learning

The first way is through *informal learning*, the multitude of ways we learn outside of classes. Humans have had access to this method probably as long as we've been conscious, being able to learn from experience, from each other, and from traditions and stories. The Industrial Revolution amplified informal learning with the mass production of media artifacts, starting with print, then moving on to audio (radio, recordings) and video (movies, television). The library profession arose to help preserve and render access to these materials. By 1985—the date of our hypothetical class from chapters 1 and 2—we were able to learn enormous amounts outside of schools.

The World Wide Web took informal learning's growth from an arithmetic curve to an exponential one. We produced and shared—often freely—huge amounts of information through documents and personal connection. Famously, the web changed the nature of media participation, as the generally passive audience mutated into a hybrid of media producer and consumer. Indeed, we now face the problem of *too much* information and too many opportunities to learn. On top of that, new and improving technologies expanded our ability to connect with each other through digital mediation: voice calls (Skype), videoconferencing, Web 2.0, and social media. We do not lack for connections to fellow learners, teachers, and pupils.

Academics produce some portion of these materials. The most rigorous form of academic writing appears in journals and monographs, often after scrutiny and improvement by other academics who peer review the material. Campus faculty and staff also produce content for general audiences, including popular nonfiction, textbooks, and interviews. Academics have gradually taken to the web to produce digital content. A casual search can easily bring up blogs, podcasts, video clips, wikis, Twitter feeds, Pinterest boards, and Second Life spaces created by academics across the disciplines. Informal learning can partake of the fruits of formal schooling.

Now, informal learning lets us follow our curiosity and start finding answers to questions. After seeing a historical movie, for example, we can Google events and people involved in the depicted period, then track down more information. Walking through a city we can use mobile phones to learn more about where we stand, perhaps taking photos or shooting video for our own reference, and someone else's. A stray comment at a bar, a politician's statement in a press conference, a singer's odd word choice, and an idea surfacing at work all give us opportunities to learn informally. The new digital world provides the means.

Informal learning does not have any necessary structure. It can be as ad hoc, apparently random, and unbounded as the learner determines. It has no formal quality control, other than the review attached to certain publications (peer-reviewed scholarship, editorially published books, and so on). It has no certain output or public status. Informal learning is formal learning's anarchist sibling.

Online Learning

The second means for accessing university-level teaching without journeying to a campus is through *online learning*, what we once called distance learning. Unlike informal learning, online classes are formally structured and offered by some kind of credentialed authority. Classes include a mix of media and technologies depending on the provider, and can include discussion boards, e-reserves, audio lectures, video presentations, audio or video meetings, the various functions an LMS offers, and whatever social media services instructor or students select.

A growing number of colleges and universities now offer a burgeoning amount of online classes. Brick-and-mortar institutions have mounted programs like Penn State's World Campus and Open SUNY, which translate face-to-face classes to online versions. Several have used the online opportunity to expand their reach and experiment with new ways of learning, as have the University of Central Florida and Southern New Hampshire University. New institutions have appeared solely for conducting online learning, including the University of Phoenix.

Online classes offer learners scheduling and access flexibility beyond that offered by brick-and-mortar campuses. Most class content is available asynchronously, so that students can arrange interaction time around their work, family, and other obligation schedules. A chance conversation brought this home to me in early 2014. I was dining at a restaurant with senior administrators from a public university. These deans and vice presidents were discussing the strengths and limitations of online learning, and one expressed skepticism of the value of schedule flexibility. Our server, plates in hand, then entered the conversation: "Oh, I disagree. Being able to fit classes into my life made all the difference for me. Getting the right classes on campus was hard, given my work hours and raising a child. Do you mind my interruption?" We didn't, and she went on to describe a not-atypical academic path. After graduating from high school, the server wanted to attend college but had problems combining class with the necessity of work. Costs, too, were an issue. The arrival of her first child kept her further away from campus. Years went by, and the advent of online classes gave her the chance to resume study.

One charge often raised against online learning is that the quality of student-instructor interaction may be less than the best of what face-to-face teaching offers. It's a fair criticism, given the greater emotional and interpersonal range being in the same room affords, as compared to even the most advanced and well-used online parallels. And yet there are limits to this complaint. It assumes an excellence in the face-to-face classroom which, to be honest, is not always the case. The reader can probably recall classes she or he has attended which featured poor pedagogy, hostile instructors, inhospitable discussion environments, opaque communications, or other failings. Furthermore, if online learning costs less than the face-to-face alternative, some learners may well be willing to accept a decrease in quality for the cost differential. Moreover, it is possible that we will see online learning improving more rapidly than brick-and-mortar education does, given the relative newness of the venue and the famously brisk pace of technological innovation (Shirky, 2012).

Open Education

We can identify a third means of off-campus learning that lives in the nexus between the previous two. Some online informal learning materials and some online classes claim or are categorized as *open education* materials or practices. Definitions of *open* are several and can contradict each other. At one end of a continuum, *open* means "easily and freely accessible," as in YouTube videos viewable by anyone with an Internet connection and (often) free web browser. At the other end, *open* denotes materials explicitly shared with the intention to allow users to freely not only consume but manipulate that content. Licenses, such as those from the Creative Commons initiative, help in declaring an item *open* in this sense. The ability to reuse, repurpose, and remix open content fits under this meaning as well. That would rule out YouTube videos in most cases, as those are streaming rather than downloadable, but would rule in blog content, MP3 files, images, and so on. Across all these definitions is the shared sense that open educational materials should be free to the learner.

Open educational materials afford that obvious yet still underappreciated economic benefit, especially as textbook prices soar and irk recession-era students. This financial virtue has led to a series of public projects, including government-supported efforts to produce open textbooks (from the state of Washington [www.openwa.org]) and open archival materials (like the Flickr [n.d.] Commons). They also offer the pedagogical benefit of deeper use, reuse, and remixing, since learners can edit content, add to or subtract from it, and return to the materials later on. Students can choose not to be passive consumers of open materials, but active users and even cocreators.

New Forms of Online Learning

A fourth method of off-campus learning appears when we consider *new forms of online learning* that have emerged. Many initial uses of technological innovation begin by transferring practices from older platforms, as when early movies imitated stage plays. Yet over time new uses appear, taking advantage of the new environment. For example, in the transition from producing stage plays to making films, directors learned to add special effects unique to celluloid and to move the camera, opening up new ways of seeing beyond what the theater-goer would have perceived. Online learning has been going through a similar process, as we began by copying offline practices, most notably the lecture, into the new medium.

Now new forms and practices have appeared, based on what the web uniquely affords. Most MOOCs draw on older ways of doing distance learning, again with the lecture. But MOOCs then scaled up the class from dozens or hundreds to thousands, then hundreds of thousands, depending on the web's power to scale. A subset of the MOOC phenomenon takes this even further, as cMOOCs (*c* for Canadian or Connectivist, pointing to the first MOOC on connectivist learning theory, created by two Canadians) emphasize social media. In cMOOCs such as DS106 or Phonar, for example, participants create content and share it over wikis, blogs, and Twitter, cocreating discussions and projects. It is learning along the lines of Wikipedia topical development or blogospheric discussion, a very different experience than that afforded by LMSs and traditional distance learning.

At least two virtual institutions have launched to scale up this kind of web-mediated collaborative learning. Peer 2 Peer University (P2PU; https://p2pu.org) is not so much a campus as a platform or marketplace for teachers and learners to find each other. Much as anyone can start a blog, podcast, or wiki, anyone with expertise to share can fire up a class on P2PU. The lack of hierarchy beyond the very limited assignment of roles points P2PU in the direction of what some call co-learning or peeragogy (Rheingold, Corneli, & Danoff, 2015). For instance, *The Peeragogy Handbook* (Rheingold et al., 2015) is organized and produced in a co-learning fashion, involving a distributed, nonhierarchical team. The University of the People (http://uopeople.edu) also supports peer-to-peer learning, while adding a somewhat traditional apparatus of trustees and course catalog. P2PU is free of charge, while the University of the People charges very low prices, depending on the student's ability to pay.

Hands-On Learning

Some of these new forms for online learning are actually based in offline activity, but require the Internet to function. The maker movement, for example, is based on celebrating and developing hands-on work. Makers create with wood, plastic, yarn, sheet metal, car parts, and old toys—anything tangible and potentially productive. Instead of a classroom, there are makerspaces, which are more like studios crossed with machine shops than traditional schoolrooms (see http://makezine.com). This is very interesting pedagogically, as makers typically learn in a nonhierarchical, cooperative environment, where teaching and learning roles are often informal and even intertwined. Makers also engage with the community by learning skills and crafts known by people beyond the education system. Indeed, making is also a way of reaching into history, as certain skills predate the web, if not the Industrial Age.

And yet technology matters for the maker movement. Makers often share their work, their plans, recipes, and reflections on the web through YouTube videos (sometimes called *instructables*), blog posts, Facebook updates, Flickr photos, and so on. These contributions to the universe of informal learning, and sometimes to the world of open education content, then help learners in their own efforts. Digital technology, particularly social media, connect individual makers to each other. Some maker projects require digital technology, such as robotics, but the more important role technology plays is an information and connective one. The use of technology in the maker movement is in this way akin to the flipped classroom, which often requires students to self-direct their learning outside of the classroom by watching videos, engaging with digital tutorials, or interacting with instruction online in other ways, and then to convene as a class prepared to discuss the instruction.

Conclusion

In short, would-be learners now have access to a variety of means for learning without physically attending a campus. Informal learning lets us follow curiosity where it leads, taking advantage of the immense and ever-expanding universe of materials. Online learning, formerly known as distance learning, gives students scheduling flexibility while drawing on steadily developing technologies and practices. Open education reduces barriers to access and can enhance learners' connection with material. And new forms of online learning have appeared.

At this point we have a better grasp of the emerging possibilities for the future of higher education, and can now turn to ways of preparing for them in the present.

Chapter 5
Campus of the Future

The world of postsecondary education is clearly changing in key ways, offering new opportunities that were not available a generation ago. How can we best prepare ourselves for these options? By *we*, I'd like to consider high school students and their families, adult learners, taxpayers who help fund public education, secondary school teachers, policymakers, and voters.

To begin, many preparatory strategies seem likely to still be valuable. For traditional-age students, developing a fine academic record and extracurricular portfolio still makes sense, especially if applying to a physical campus. Policymakers and voters continue to need to scrutinize public education finances and structures. Teachers and parents are required to teach critical thinking and soft skills of interpersonal relations and socialization. Researching postsecondary learning venues is perhaps more valuable than ever, given the diversity of new options and possible threats to the old.

Against that familiar background, the biggest change is taking online learning seriously. Learners of all ages should consider virtual classes for the advantages they can offer: scheduling flexibility, lower costs, different curricula, and new forms of teaching. At the present time, some of those class experiences are not as high quality as some face-to-face, on-campus ones; given that, potential students should weigh cost, convenience, and quality as tradeoffs.

We should also get ready to take off-campus learning more seriously. Informal learning may gain in social value, especially if underemployment gives people more free time than they anticipated and if we continue to fear the costs and benefits of formal education. Alternative forms of online learning are likely to develop and expand. Unless we solve the cost/benefit problem for postsecondary education, we are likely to explore alternatives. Clayton Christensen, Curtis Johnson, and Michael Horn (2008) see this as a classic disruptive opportunity in which low-cost, low-quality alternatives outflank established enterprises (brick-and-mortar institutions).

I'm not wholly convinced, but I do see an American population looking for ways around the current sense of crisis.

Preparing for Learning After High School

Let us assume you are a high school student, a high school student's family, an educator of high school students, or a combination of these. What are the ways forward into these new worlds?

Identifying and reflecting on students' areas of interest and their strengths provide starting points for exploring options for education beyond high school. Years of K–12 school plus years of informal learning give students a sense of what they are interested in and what aptitudes they have: astronomy, building cars, dentistry, entrepreneurship, facilitating groups. This knowledge has surfaced by all kinds of external means, as they have been graded, tested, assessed, recommended, or dissuaded by teachers. Students have also learned about their mind by developing it over time and reflecting on its performance. They know what parts of the academic and adult worlds they like, and which they would shun, given the opportunity.

Moreover, and this may be harder to grasp, students also have a sense of how they learn. Think back to when you wrote an excellent paper when you were a student. What were the conditions for its composition? Did you write better alone or in groups? Did you proceed best starting from an outline or just writing flat out? Remember the subjects you recall with greatest clarity. Was it because of lectures or discussion? Compare with the ways you learned outside of school. Put these together and you are starting to understand the best ways you learn. That's vital knowledge, as it can help you learn better in the future.

Making Choices About Higher Education and Other Pathways

With self-knowledge in mind, students who are graduating or otherwise exiting high school are well-equipped to consider the next stage. Residential higher education is one possibility, potentially giving a variety of benefits. They can pursue those interests at a higher level, testing themselves to see if they can carry them into the adult world. Students can also explore other topics, expanding their mind and perhaps leading them down new pathways. As residential students, they are also studying how to live on their own: managing money, building new friendships, coping with stresses, falling in love, learning a new town or city. Campuses maintain services to help students with all of these learning experiences; be sure to request them.

Financially, things now get interesting. You might start loading up with student loans; two-thirds of students do, and their average debt is around $30,000. This may daunt you, and it is the highest amount of student debt incurred in U.S. history (Board of Governors of the Federal Reserve System, 2014). On the flip side, though, history teaches us that once you graduate, you'll generally make more money—up to half a million dollars more—than if you did not. In that context, student loans are a fine investment.

Two cautions. First, note that I said *generally*. Not all degrees pay equally over a person's life. Second, not everyone graduates, but everyone borrowing still must pay that debt back. Going to college, not graduating, and holding debt is a bad combination.

Some students decide to attend multiple institutions in order to keep costs down. This can include taking classes at a community college, transferring to a state university, while also taking online classes elsewhere. Assembling credits toward a degree this way resembles Lego bricks, and is nicknamed "swirling" by higher education administrators. Another cost control tactic is living at home and attending a nearby campus, rather than living on campus or setting up an apartment.

Let's take another tack. Perhaps higher education isn't the right choice at this time in a student's life. There are very good reasons why this might be so. First, the student has probably spent nearly his or her entire thinking life in school, thirteen years, more or less. Perhaps the student might want to spend more time in the nonschool world. Who is this person when he or she is not a student?

Second, recollect the student's interests and aptitudes. Is a university the best fit for him or her? If the student's strengths lean towards hands-on work, many fields beckon these days. Woodworking, plumbing, electrical work, and others are seeing their workers age right towards retirement. As a result wages are rising. He or she might be better off avoiding university, at least for now, in order to develop a career and make some money.

Alternatively, the student might want to start a business. Entrepreneurship calls deeply to some of us, offering the chance to change the world and support oneself, if not strike it rich. The student may already have identified an unmet need and want to fulfill it with a startup. In this case, he or she could explore business incubators, outfits designed to help ideas become enterprises. Students might try out for the very competitive Thiel Fellowship (www.thielfellowship.org), which pays them to do just this. They could also consider other entrepreneur-supportive entities, like the San Francisco-based HackerHouse (http://hackerhouse.info).

What if none of these appeal to students, as they honestly have no idea what they want to do with their lives? Then maybe they should take some time to figure this out. If they have the resources, take time off to explore the world, looking for a sense of who they are. Or consider a very student-centered college, like a liberal arts campus, which are terrific places to conduct this kind of self-exploration. They provide multiple pathways for students' minds to explore, and offer a very supportive environment. The Colleges That Change Lives (www.ctcl.org) list is a good place to start. Or arrange to spend time developing interests and strengths through other alternatives like makerspaces and online classes.

Skills for Learning Beyond K–12

If, on the other hand, students are not yet done with high school, then they can work on skills to prepare themselves for that big transition. Many K–12 systems try hard to teach those skills, but fall short for various reasons, including budget cuts, having to hire new people, and limited skillsets.

What should students work on? The following are some options.

- **Multimedia skills:** Turn yourself from a media consumer to a media maker. Pick a medium you especially appreciate (video, audio, games) and start learning how to make these products. There are many online resources that can help, including tutorials and teachers. Share what you make. Tell stories with these new tools.

- **Coding:** The languages that make computers accomplish things in the world are clearly powerful areas for learning. If your high school doesn't teach programming or you've exceeded what it offers, turn to the different sources of education we've mentioned so far—online learning, informal learning, open education, and new ways to learn online, like Codecademy (www.codecademy.com). If you don't mind trying kids' things, download and learn Scratch (https://scratch.mit.edu), a famously useful basic coding introduction. Also, look into what your local and regional community and technical colleges offer.

- **Robotics:** Automation is advancing in the world, and robots carry a large part of that transformative power. If you haven't built a robot, start with Lego Mindstorms, a well-designed teaching system. Or look into working on drones, a very influential part of the robot world, and very accessible to learners. YouTube videos provide abundant avenues to explore work with drones and easily show learners how to get started.

- **Social media literacy:** Learn how best to take advantage of the online world by practicing curation, the careful accumulation (and regular weeding of) useful feeds. Decide when to participate in exchanges. Explore a platform in great detail.

- **Your online self:** Figure out how people find you online through Googling and other methods, and work to improve that impression to your liking. A key step in this process is creating your own web domain (Udell, 2012). Compare the different worlds of anonymous forums like Yik Yak (www.yikyakapp.com) with the detailed description of yourself available on the rest of the web.

If students follow several of these paths, they will become more knowledgeable about the online world, and better able to interact with it. These skills will help them learn in general, and also teach them more about their aptitudes, their interests, and how they learn.

High schools are actually well placed to help students with these avenues to learning. Many have built up computing capabilities since the 1990s, relying on federal E-Rate funds and a general sense of urgency that students become technologically competent. All schools have some network capability, a collection of computers, and access to IT support. Funding issues cause quality and quantity to vary massively (see the following sections), but the basics are generally available, especially in the wake of Common Core testing requirements. Moreover, public libraries provide a heroic and underappreciated service in offering access to all comers. Additionally, cell phones offer a third access route to the web.

Given these options, schools can help teenagers progress in preparing themselves technologically for postsecondary education. Perhaps the most challenging part of this is creating the right curriculum and either retraining or hiring new teachers to instruct it.

Considerations for Adult Learners

What if you aren't a teenager, but an adult learner seeking to resume learning at the postsecondary level? Some of the preceding advice doesn't apply to you, most likely. You probably don't need to spend time learning how to live on your own. If you have a job or family, you might not be able to take time off to explore the world or your mind.

Yet the other items may apply very well to your current situation. The range of postsecondary schooling options we discussed is also open to you, although the residential liberal arts experience probably isn't a good fit. Brick-and-mortar institutions have powerful advantages, as do online learning institutions. Informal and new forms of learning may also meet your needs.

Our list of useful technology practices and skills applies to you as well. Many people expect teenagers to have digital native abilities; those expectations are lower, the older you are. Defy them by picking up advantages by immersing yourself in these technologies.

Building Capacity for New Forms of Learning

Although there are many more options for continuing education beyond K–12 than there have been in the past, we can only take advantage of these new forms of learning if we possess the requisite capacities. Broadband adoption remains uneven in the United States, and is especially thin on the ground in rural and poor areas. While public libraries have performed important roles in connecting people to the

Internet, far too many remain offline or struggle with access speeds, rendering the online world a problematic place to visit. Mobile phone access makes up for these gaps in some areas, but even advanced smartphones are not full replacements for laptop or desktop access. Think of users with limited vision, and the problems of typing an essay.

A larger obstacle concerns skills. As these technologies advance, not all Americans are ready to take advantage of them, even as some tools become easier to use. To some extent this is based on generational difference—yes, it's an easy stereotype to see old folks fumbling with tech, while kids use it with ease—but repeated Pew Internet and American Life studies show clear gaps by age for many technologies. Skill differences also open up based on varying access to technologies, which ethnicity, socioeconomic class, and rural location can shape. If we want to open up online learning for all Americans, we need to take steps to make sure they have the capacity to take advantage of it. This involves policies and practices, such as:

- Increasing K–12 teacher training on how to teach with technology
- Launching public and private services to teach seniors about new technologies
- Expanding broadband to include underserved communities. This may involve public funds, Internet service providers identifying new business opportunities, or the implementation of new technologies, like Google's Project Loon (www.google.com/loon)
- Content providers (textbook creators, faculty course designers, and so on) providing mobile-friendly versions of their work. Responsive design is an especially rewarding option here, publishing web content so that it detects a user's device type and reformats itself to the best format

Schooling in the New Gilded Age

The largest obstacle we face in preparing generations of U.S. citizens for higher education goes beyond technologies and workshops. We are now a society deeply divided by economic inequality. As Piketty (2014) devastatingly demonstrates, our class separations have regressed to Gilded Age levels, and seem likely to deepen. As Robert Putnam (2015) argues, we are reshaping neighborhoods and socialization to enforce segregation by wealth. Racial difference can worsen this, as blacks and Latinos face generally lower socioeconomic status and racism. U.S. women remain drastically underrepresented in technology, a minority status enforced by sexism both structural and explicit, as the 2015 Gamergate scandal reveals (Straumsheim, 2015).

These bitter inequalities matter deeply when we consider the intersection of education and technology, and we are at best foolish to ignore them. To begin, U.S. K–12 school funding is largely driven by hyperlocal financing. This generally means that the wealthiest school districts often fund their primary and secondary schools well, while the poorest underfund theirs. This leads to well-known achievement gaps in a variety of metrics, from scores on multiple tests across all grades to graduation levels and college placement. The nonwealthy, nonwhite populations are not so well prepared for higher education as their gated community neighbors are. They are also not as well-educated in using digital technologies. There are exceptions to these trends, of course, as some wealthy districts underfund their schools for various reasons, and some poor areas produce splendid schools. But the general tendencies hold true often enough to change the face of education.

This structural difference in higher education preparation yields another challenge. Students from the wealthiest families tend to be the ones best poised to take advantage of online learning. They tend to have greater awareness of the education system, and more confidence in navigating it, than their poorer peers who are more likely to be first-generation college students. The wealthiest families tend to include multiple generations of university students. This experiential difference gives them a leg up in understanding a new class environment, seeking help, or navigating bureaucracy. Call it scholastic literacy, if you like, and not having solid amounts of it can make apprehending and succeeding in education additionally difficult. We can see an example of this in MOOC research that reveals the learners most likely to take advantage of those online classes are adults already equipped with some degree of higher education (Hollands & Tirthali, 2014).

Economic differences play out in the funding and functioning of colleges and universities, as well. Community colleges, which educate nearly one-half of all postsecondary students, cost far less than other institutions and receive fewer resources than others. Many of their teaching staff are adjuncts. In contrast, elite research universities and liberal arts colleges publish the highest tuition charges, while sometimes offering the greatest campus amenities and, most importantly, excellent teaching. The wealthiest universities have endowments in the billions, amounts so large that Piketty considers their impact on the U.S. economy—not on the education sector alone, but as concentrations of wealth so massive that they could by themselves possibly increase wealth inequality for the entire nation (Piketty, 2014). Liberal arts institutions often feature low student-instructor ratios, and rely on tenured, full-time, passionate teachers to support students in their learning careers. In contrast, public colleges and universities, often called "state schools," experience an ongoing reduction in state funding (Newfield, 2008).

Overcoming Educational Segregation

In short, we're approaching a situation where the wealthiest families tend to send their students to the best-resourced K–12 schools, then onward to the wealthiest and highest-quality colleges and universities. The reverse is also true. America is looking ahead to educational segregation.

If that's in the future, then a perverse result may appear. Students with the best academic preparation will take advantage of the best education face-to-face teaching has to offer, while underprepared, under-resourced students turn to alternatives they have been ill equipped to seize.

If this comes to pass, the policy and practice recommendations I offered in this chapter will not address the fundamental problem of deepening, determining inequality. They might help mitigate the chasm to a degree, but ultimately fall short.

In response, I can offer three possible ways forward.

1. **Technological advancement:** Tools for learning develop rapidly in ease of use, becoming friendly for adult and traditional learners alike. Intelligent assistants—not Microsoft's notorious Clippy nor the more advanced Siri, but the next stage of software helpers—could serve as tutoring aids, if not as tutors themselves. We can think of this as Young Lady's Illustrated Primer future, named for a plot in Neal Stephenson's 1995 novel *The Diamond Age*. In that science fiction future, an intelligent ebook teaches a cadre of poor girls a variety of skills, leading to their self-organization into a social movement. The primer might not be exactly what the Gates Foundation has in mind, but technological advancement as a solution to these nontechnological problems is what they and others are investing in.

2. **Progressive social policies:** We could see a return to the early 20th-century progressive movement, with politicians embracing powerful policy means to challenge deep economic inequality. At the federal level, Congress could, in theory, return income and wealth tax rates to mid-20th century heights, then redistribute those funds into social programs. States could follow suit. In terms of education, those states could reform K–12 financing so as to level out differences between towns, along the lines of Vermont's Act 60. That 1997 law, the Equal Educational Opportunity Act, reformatted school financing to a uniform state level, and has worked ever since. This neoprogressive moment may seem implausible in 2015, but it could well follow a sustained movement of popular resentment against extravagant inequality.

3. **Fallout from the bubble model and peak education:** If the bubble model proves accurate, or if peak education transpires, then education prices should fall, and the number of students drop. This could have a silver lining of making those reduced colleges and universities more accessible to students, as tuition and fees become more affordable, and as campuses try harder to attract students. Without the kind of social policy reforms mentioned previously, inequalities would persist, but at least higher education would be less distanced from the 99 percent.

The scale of changes represented by these three futures indicates just how deeply laid are these challenges for America's education system. The size of their transformations also indicates the full range of possibility we must bear in mind if we are to realistically prepare for the future of higher education. In terms of Wayne Gretzky's famous adage, the puck is skidding across a lot of ice. It isn't likely to follow one single path that we can anticipate easily.

Guiding Social and Technological Transformation

Let me conclude by bringing these enormous questions of social and technological transformation back to the scale of families and individual decision makers. These major themes have clear implications at the personal level.

Technology

Learning more about digital technologies is likely to benefit nearly every person reading this book. Students will be better placed to learn more content more effectively, while attaining a deeper understanding about an analog world continually redesigned by the digital. Policymakers and school leaders will also obtain that understanding.

The Traditional Campus

Higher education institutions still exist, and most (if not all) are likely to persist over the next decade (at least), barring catastrophe. These campuses are changing from their 20th century forms, and we must prepare for their new shapes. That means learning how to learn from technology-mediated classes, benefitting from open learning, and educating ourselves in networks.

Learning Alternatives

There is a good chance that alternatives to the traditional classroom will flourish in the near- and medium-term future. We all have the chance of taking advantage of these new learning venues, from cMOOCs to co-learning. We may decide to combine alternatives with traditional education, or to just select one. Americans may decide that college as we once knew it is not for everyone, but informal learning will continue and grow.

Politics

Higher education is the subject of intense attention from state and federal governments. As of this writing, the bipartisan consensus on education reform remains strong, and that will help guide campus changes into the future. At the same time, public outrage over racial, economic, and gender inequalities seems to be rising. This could lead to a new politics of education, one which might seek to redress these issues, or take a different path entirely. The point is that higher education is now very politicized, and we need to take those politics under consideration when planning the future of a family, a township, a campus, or one's own career.

Conclusion

Through all of these changes we can glimpse one reason for optimism. Learners now have access to more resources, more teachers, and more fellow students than ever before. This is a splendid environment for the curious mind to inhabit. How we structure that environment, what new shapes higher education takes, what learning becomes . . . answering those questions are the task that lies ahead. It's a task we hold in common, so let us hope our new abilities to inform ourselves guide us wisely.

References

Alexander, B. (2009, May 28). Apprehending the future: Emerging technologies, from science fiction to campus reality. *EDUCAUSE Review, 44*(3). Accessed at www.educause.edu/ero/article/apprehending-future-emerging-technologies-scienc-fiction-campus-reality on March 20, 2015.

Alexander, B. (2013, September 18). *Peak education 2013.* Accessed at http://bryanalexander.org/2013/09/18/peak-education-2013 on March 20, 2015.

Alexander, B. (2014a). *Future trends in technology and education.* Accessed at http://ftte.us on March 18, 2015.

Alexander, B. (2014b, April 7). Has higher ed peaked? *Inside Higher Ed.* Accessed at www.insidehighered.com/views/2014/04/07/essay-considers-whether-higher-education-us-has-peaked on March 20, 2015.

Arum, R., & Roksa, J. (2011). *Academically adrift: Limited learning on college campuses.* Chicago: University of Chicago Press.

Atomic object technology showcase. (2015). Allendale, MI: Grand Valley State University. Accessed at www.gvsu.edu/techshowcase on March 20, 2015.

Barnard, C. (Producer), Farrey, N. (Producer), & Jonze, S. (Director). (2013). *Her* [Motion picture]. United States: Warner Brothers.

Board of Governors of the Federal Reserve System. (2014, June 5). *Consumer credit–G.19* [Statistical release]. Accessed at http://federalreserve.gov/releases/g19/current/default.htm on August 11, 2014.

Bureau of Labor Statistics. (2014). *Occupational outlook handbook: Most new jobs.* Accessed at www.bls.gov/ooh/most-new-jobs.htm on March 20, 2015.

Bureau of Labor Statistics. (2015, July). *Economic news release: Employment situation summary.* Accessed at www.bls.gov/news.release/empsit.nr0.htm on August 7, 2015.

Changing patterns in U.S. immigration and population. (2014, December 18). [Issue brief]. Washington, DC: Pew Charitable Trusts. Accessed at www.pewtrusts.org/en/research-and-analysis/issue-briefs/2014/12/changing-patterns-in-us-immigration-and-population on December 18, 2014.

Christensen, C., Johnson, C.W., & Horn, M. B. (2008). *Disrupting class: How disruptive innovation will change the way the world learns.* New York: McGraw-Hill.

Combe, P. (2013, June 3). We've let student loans become a horror story … now is time to face it. *The New England Journal of Higher Education.* Accessed at www.nebhe.org/thejournal/weve-let-student-loans-become-a-horror-story-nows-time-to-face-it/ on July 6, 2015.

Delbanco, A. (2012). *College: What it was, is, and should be.* Princeton, NJ: Princeton University Press.

DeLong, B. (2013, December 11). *Well, it's the end of Nicholas Dirks's first semester as Berkeley Chancellor, so why not offer him some unsolicited advice?* Accessed at http://blogs.berkeley.edu/2013/12/11/well-its-the-end-of-nicholas-dirkss-first-semester-as-berkeley-chancellor-so-why-not-offer-him-some-unsolicited-advice on March 20, 2015.

Department of Philosophy, San José State University. (2013, May 2). An open letter to Professor Michael Sandel from the Philosophy Department at San Jose State U. *The Chronicle of Higher Education.* Accessed at http://chronicle.com/article/The-Document-Open-Letter-From/138937 on July 3, 2015.

de Vise, D. (2012, April 22). At Virginia Tech, computers help solve a math class problem. *Washington Post.* Accessed at www.washingtonpost.com/local/education/at-virginia-tech-computers-help-solve-a-math-class-problem/2012/04/22/gIQAmAOmaT_story.html on March 20, 2015.

Doug Engelbart Institute. (n.d.). *Doug's 1968 demo.* Accessed at www.dougengelbart.org/firsts/dougs-1968-demo.html on March 20, 2015.

Erickson, A. (2013, September 4). *Why fewer students in college is good for the economy.* Accessed at www.citylab.com/politics/2013/09/why-fewer-students-college-good-economy/6764 on March 20, 2015.

Fain, P. (2015, March 20). Texas-size math lab. *Inside Higher Ed.* Accessed at www.insidehighered.com/news/2015/03/20/austin-community-colleges-promising-experiment-personalized-remedial-mathematics on March 23, 2015.

Field, K. (2015, March 16). Education Dept. considers creating not 1 but 2 college-ratings systems. *Chronicle of Higher Education.* Accessed at http://chronicle.com/article/Education-Dept-Considers/228531 on March 17, 2015.

Finkle, V., & Peters, A. (2012, March 30). U.S. bank, Chase pull back from student lending. *American Banker.* Accessed at www.americanbanker.com/issues/177_63/us-bank-student-lending-cfpb-1048016-1.html on March 20, 2015.

Flickr. (n.d.). *The commons.* Accessed at flickr.com/commons on March 20, 2015.

Gold, M. K. (Ed.). (2012). *Debates in the digital humanities.* Minneapolis: University of Minnesota Press.

Gonzales, L. M., Allum, J. R., & Sowell, R. S. (2013, September). *Graduate enrollment and degrees: 2002 to 2012*. Accessed at http://cgsnet.org/ckfinder/userfiles/files/GEDReport_2012.pdf on March 20, 2015.

Hollands, F. M., & Tirthali, D. (2014). MOOCs: *Expectations and reality* (Full Report). New York: Center for Benefit-Cost Studies of Education, Teachers College, Columbia University. Accessed at http://cbcse.org/wordpress/wp-content/uploads/2014/05/MOOCs_Expectations_and_Reality.pdf on July 6, 2015.

Hough, L. (2014, January 14). Brennan by design. *Harvard Ed Magazine*. Accessed at www.gse.harvard.edu/news/ed/14/01/brennan-design on March 20, 2015.

Jaschik, S. (2013, September 18). Feeling the heat: The 2013 survey of college and university admissions directors. *Inside Higher Ed*. Accessed at www.insidehighered.com/news/survey/feeling-heat-2013-survey-college-and-university-admissions-directors on March 20, 2015.

Johnson, L., Becker, S. A., Estrada, V., & Freeman, A. (2015). *NMC Horizon Report: 2015 higher education edition*. Austin, TX: The New Media Consortium. Accessed at www.nmc.org/publication/nmc-horizon-report-2015-higher-education-edition on March 20, 2015.

Khazan, O. (2014, September 30). The recession's baby bust. *The Atlantic*. Accessed at www.theatlantic.com/business/archive/2014/09/the-recessions-baby-bust/380909 on September 30, 2014.

Kiley, K. (2013, July 23). Holding the line. *Inside Higher Ed*. Accessed at www.insidehighered.com/news/2013/07/23/salle-mae-survey-finds-families-unwilling-pay-more-higher-education on March 20, 2015.

Kitroeff, N. (2015, July 1). Is it time to start shutting down law schools? *Bloomberg News*. Accessed at www.bloomberg.com/news/articles/2015-07-01/is-it-time-to-start-shutting-down-law-schools on July 4, 2015.

Kleiner Perkins leads $20M Series C for Duolingo. (2014, February 18). *EdSurge*. Accessed at www.edsurge.com/n/2014-02-18-kleiner-perkins-leads-20m-series-c-for-duolingo on July 3, 2015.

Kurtzleben, D. (2013, October 23). CHARTS: Just how fast has college tuition grown? *US News and World Report*. Accessed at www.usnews.com/news/articles/2013/10/23/charts-just-how-fast-has-college-tuition-grown on July 6, 2015.

Leonard, E. (2015). *Great expectations: Students and video in higher education* [White paper]. Accessed at www.sagepub.com/repository/binaries/pdfs/StudentsandVideo.pdf on March 20, 2015.

Lorin, J. (2014a, February 25). Dwindling midwest high school grads spur college hunt. *Bloomberg News*. Accessed at www.bloomberg.com/news/2014-02-25/dwindling-midwest-high-school-grads-spur-college-applicant-hunt.html on July 5, 2015.

Lorin, J. (2014b, February 3). Harvard freshman applications drop 2.1% as Midwest leads decline. *Bloomberg News.* Accessed at www.bloomberg.com/news/2014-02-03/harvard-freshman-applications-drop-2-1-as-midwest-leads-decline.html on July 5, 2015.

McCarthy, J. (2015, June 23). Americans view quality of two-year, four-year colleges similarly. *Gallup.* Accessed at www.gallup.com/poll/183779/americans-view-quality-two-year-four-year-colleges-similarly.aspx on July 2, 2015.

Newfield, C. (2008). *Unmaking the public university: the forty-year assault on the middle class.* Cambridge, MA: Harvard University Press.

Patten, E., & Fry, R. (2015). *How millennials today compare with their grandparents 50 years ago.* Washington, DC: Pew Research Center. Accessed at www.pewresearch.org/fact-tank/2015/03/19/how-millennials-compare-with-their-grandparents on March 20, 2015.

Perez, S. (2015, February 17). Wells Fargo loans increase as yields decline. *Market Realist.* Accessed at http://marketrealist.com/2015/02/wells-fargo-loans-increase-yields-decline on March 20, 2015.

Pérez-Peña, R. (2013, July 25). College enrollment falls as economy recovers. *New York Times.* Accessed at www.nytimes.com/2013/07/26/education/in-a-recovering-economy-a-decline-in-college-enrollment.html?pagewanted=all&_r=0 on March 20, 2015.

Piketty, T. (2014). *Capital in the twenty-first century* (A. Goldhammer, Trans.). Cambridge, MA: Harvard University Press.

Putnam, R. (2015). *Our kids: The American dream in crisis.* New York: Simon and Schuster.

REPORT: *Current term enrollment report–Spring 2015.* (2015, May 13). Herndon, VA: National Student Clearinghouse Research Center. Accessed at http://nscresearchcenter.org/currenttermenrollmentestimate-spring2015/ on July 5, 2015.

Rheingold, H., Corneli, J., & Danoff, C. H. (2015). *The peeragogy handbook* (3rd ed.). Somerville, MA: Pierce Press.

Robinson, B. L., & Moore, A. H. (2006). Chapter 42. The math emporium: Virginia Tech. *EDUCAUSE.* Accessed at www.educause.edu/research-and-publications/books/learning-spaces/chapter-42-virginia-tech-math-emporium on March 20, 2015.

Saez, E., & Piketty, T. (2006). The evolution of top incomes: A historical and international perspective. *American Economic Review, Papers and Proceedings, 96*(2), 200–205. Accessed at http://eml.berkeley.edu/~saez/piketty-saezAEAPP06.pdf on March 15, 2015.

Scully, M. (2015). B of A bids adieu to its student loans (or does it?). *American Banker*. Accessed at www.americanbanker.com/news/national-regional/b-of-a-bids-adieu-to-its-student-loans-or-does-it-1072491–1.html on March 20, 2015.

Shirky, C. (2012, November 12). *Napster, Udacity, and the academy*. Accessed at www.shirky.com/weblog/2012/11/napster-udacity-and-the-academy on March 20, 2015.

Shulman, J. L., & Bowen, W. G. (2002). *The game of life: College sports and educational values*. Princeton, NJ: Princeton University Press.

Singer, N. (2015, January 11). Silicon Valley turns its eye to education. *New York Times*. Accessed at www.nytimes.com/2015/01/12/technology/silicon-valley-turns-its-eye-to-education.html on January 14, 2015.

Stephenson, N. (1995). *The diamond age*. New York: Bantam Books.

Stratford, M. (2015). Upping the ante on free. *Inside Higher Ed*. Accessed at www.insidehighered.com/news/2015/02/20/bernie-sanders-calls-two-tuition-free-years-all-public-colleges-and-universities on March 20, 2015.

Straumsheim, C. (2015, April 28). Gaming beyond Gamergate. *Inside Higher Ed*. Accessed at www.insidehighered.com/news/2015/04/28/women-gaming-discuss-role-academics-understanding-gamergate on July 6, 2015.

Summers, L. H. (2014, February 24). U.S. economic prospects: Secular stagnation, hysteresis, and the zero lower bound. Keynote address at the National Association for Business Economics Policy Conference. *Business Economics, 49*(2), 65–73. Accessed at http://larrysummers.com/wp-content/uploads/2014/06/NABE-speech-Lawrence-H.-Summers1.pdf on July 6, 2015.

Taleb, N. N. (2007). *The black swan: The impact of the highly improbable*. New York: Random House.

Taylor, P. (2014, April 10). *Two dramas in slow motion*. Washington, DC: Pew Research Center. Accessed at www.pewresearch.org/next-america/#Two-Dramas-in-Slow-Motion on July 2, 2015.

Udell, J. (2012, July). A domain of one's own. *Wired*. Accessed at www.wired.com/2012/07/a-domain-of-ones-own/ on March 20, 2015.

Vinge, V. (2006). *Rainbows end*. New York: Tor.

Weaver, J. B. (2014, January 13). *Remaking higher education: The maker lab at Abilene Christian University*. Accessed at www.ideaslaboratory.com/post/93343635798/remaking-higher-education-the-maker-lab-at-abilene-chris on March 20, 2015.

Weldon, D. (2014, July 2). Managing a BYOD program on steroids. *FierceCIO*. Accessed at www.fiercecio.com/story/managing-byod-program-steroids/2014-07-02 on March 20, 2015.

Solutions for Modern Learning

Solutions Series: Solutions for Modern Learning engages K–12 educators in a powerful conversation about learning and schooling in the connected world. In a short, reader-friendly format, these books challenge traditional thinking about education and help to develop the modern contexts teachers and leaders need to effectively support digital learners.

Claim Your Domain—And Own Your Online Presence
Audrey Watters
BKF687

The End of School as We Know It
Bruce Dixon
BKF692

Freedom to Learn
Will Richardson
BKF688

Gearing Up for Learning Beyond K–12
Bryan Alexander
BKF693

Make School Meaningful—And Fun!
Roger C. Schank
BKF686

The New Pillars of Modern Teaching
Gayle Allen
BKF685

Wait! Your professional development journey doesn't have to end with the last pages of this book.

We realize improving student learning doesn't happen overnight. And your school or district shouldn't be left to puzzle out all the details of this process alone.

No matter where you are on the journey, we're committed to helping you get to the next stage.

Take advantage of everything from **custom workshops** to **keynote presentations** and **interactive web and video conferencing**. We can even help you develop an action plan tailored to fit your specific needs.

Let's get the conversation started.

Call 888.763.9045 today.

solution-tree.com